Pots, Pans, & Five-Year Plans

My Journey from Dishwasher to CEO

Haitham Mattar

POTS, PANS, AND FIVE-YEAR PLANS

My Journey from Dishwasher to CEO

To my late mother, who was my biggest fan, motivator,
inspiration, and always pushed me to aim higher.

To my brother Salem, for everything he did for me
in raising me and teaching me discipline, respect,
and that working hard always pays off.

To my wife and children for being with me throughout
my highs and lows and for always believing in me.

CONTENTS

CHAPTER 1

BEYOND THE DISH ROOM

I t was like a jungle in there.

The steam. The heat. The clatter and clang. The shouts, hoots and howls. The air thick with pungent scents that tickled and titillated the nose. A rush of energy and an incessant flow of activity. Moments of rest were few and far between.

This was the atmosphere in the hotel kitchen where I began what would turn into a thirty-year (and counting) career in hospitality. The intensity and rigor of those first days working as a dishwasher have stayed with me, forever tattooed on my mind.

The scene I just described came a few days into my tenure, my first time working the breakfast rush. My first day on the job, spent on the afternoon shift, was more relaxed. It was a business hotel so, at that hour, most of our guests were in the office or in meetings, giving presentations and inking deals offsite. Washing dishes for the lunch crowd was an easy foray into the job. I thought, "This is going to be smooth sailing. I can handle this."

But when I came back to work on my second day, this time for the morning shift, it was like all hell had broken loose. It was a busy 250-room hotel, which meant a couple hundred people would descend on the dining room almost simultaneously, all of them wanting breakfast, and wanting it now.

At the beginning of my shift, I looked out through the window that separated the kitchen from the dining area, and my eyes grew wide as they all converged on the buffet.

But I didn't have time to observe; more urgent matters needed tending to on my side of the window: hurried waiters screaming, dumping plates, yelling out orders to the chef. Yelling at *me*. I recall the sharp chemical smell of the detergent, and the remnants of black coffee, bacon, eggs, and syrup that clung to the dirty dishes piling up next to me. I scrubbed and cleaned pots and pans as fast as I could while feeding plates, silverware, cups, and bowls into the powerful industrial dishwasher.

In a busy kitchen, there is so much happening at once. It's a whirlwind. You try to stay focused as you're bombarded by stimuli on all sides. You're like a race car driver: dialed in, focus turned up to 100, tunnel vision, eyes locked on the road and the cars in front of you because you know one slip-up at 160 mph can be deadly.

There was no time to think; you just *did*. It was a rush that is both energizing and deflating. I was invigorated by the controlled chaos in the kitchen and by the demands of the job, but by the end of the shift around 2:00pm, I was dead. My hands were like prunes from bucket after bucket of hot water. My apron was stained like the ragged uniform of a soldier emerging from the trenches. My shoes were splattered with grease and the leftovers of people's breakfast.

And the next day, I'd have to do it all over again.

Good thing, because I loved it.

As the weeks went on, I came to appreciate the day-to-day challenges as well as the importance of our work to the smooth functioning of the restaurant and, by extension, the hotel itself. Without clean dishware, everything grinds to a halt.

Those crazy, grueling, push-yourself-to-the-limits mornings washing dishes at the Atlanta Courtyard Marriott on Delk Road was the start of a long and, if I may say so humbly, illustrious career in hotels and restaurants worldwide.

Today, I serve as a managing director with the InterContinental Hotels Group based in Dubai, running an operation of over $2 billion, more than 200 hotels and 24,000 employees. Along the way, I've held prestigious positions with Hilton Hotels Corporation, the Ras al Khaimah Tourism Development Authority in the UAE, and the Saudi Ministry of Tourism. But the foundation for my success was established in the steamy, noisy dish room. In hospitality, whether you're on the top of the totem pole or the lowest-ranking intern, you must uphold certain standards without fail: to do your job with precision, agility, attention to detail, and the utmost professionalism, integrating seamlessly with your team members (all oars rowing the same direction, as they say) and making the utmost effort to ensure the client is satisfied.

Even now as I work at the corporate level, consorting with bigwigs and collaborating on eight-figure deals, I'm still in some respects, a humble "dishwasher." I've traded the black work pants and dirty shoes for a suit and tie, and most of my work is conducted in air-conditioned board rooms and opulent banquet halls, rather than the sweaty, noisy kitchens. But my duty is the same: to be of service to others, contribute diligently to the team and fulfill my role in an intricate process that ensures the whole operation can proceed smoothly and customers can return home satisfied.

Over the past few decades, I've checked in guests in a major Atlanta business hotel, waited on rock stars in exclusive restaurants, directed marketing for a luxury hotel chain in the Middle East, traveled to Africa, Asia, Europe, and countless exotic locales in between, and dined with ministers, monarchs, and dignitaries. I've had exposure to virtually every role in the industry, and through it all I've seen the best and the worst (but mostly the best).

My broad experience has also given me exposure to the challenges the industry faces as we enter the next era of travel and tourism. Technological, geopolitical, cultural, and economic trends will reshape hospitality just as they are reshaping all facets of society—for the hotel and restaurant business is, in many ways, a microcosm of society at large. You can learn a lot about people, and human civilization more broadly, from working a few hours at reception, serving cocktails at a rooftop bar happy hour—or scrubbing pots and pans in the back room. The hotel business holds a mirror up to humanity, showing us what we excel at and what we need to improve.

I'm writing this book to share my own story, which is a kind of rags-to-riches tale that might inspire others who dare to dream big, and to provide an expert's take on hospitality, which is a business everyone comes into contact with (we've all stayed in hotels before) but few truly understand.

I'm also addressing those who are considering entering the profession. One of the challenges we face, which I'll delve into later, is an uncertain future for the next generation of workers. In order to thrive and adapt, we must attract young, hungry professionals in Generation Z and so-called Generation Alpha (those who are babies and children today). What does hospitality have to offer them? And what can they contribute to an industry that is essential to how humans live, work, and play?

The lessons I'll impart in this book, informed by my experience in almost every niche of the profession, will be particularly relevant to industry folks but also valuable for anyone who is pursuing a long-term goal, trying to make in-roads in a competitive field, or endeavoring to improve their life personally or professionally. For example, one of the themes I'll discuss is "finding your superpower": identifying that special talent you have that few others possess, and learning to leverage it to the fullest. I'll talk about maintaining grace under pressure, working through difficult moments and challenging times and learning to recognize that we often do our best work—and achieve the most growth and character-building—during dark days and trying times.

I'll discuss how to recognize opportunity when it comes, and when it's in short supply, how to *create* your own opportunities. That's something that has aided me many times during my career. And I'll discuss the value of *relationships*—how to cultivate them over time, how to be someone that others like, respect, and want to work with. Regardless of your field, that, more than virtually anything else, will make the difference between being stuck behind the bar for 20 years (not that there's anything wrong with that if that's what you wish to do) and getting promoted to the upper rungs to reap the rewards and take on fresh challenges.

The hotel industry is a cornerstone of the economy, generating nearly five *trillion* dollars worldwide,[1] and employing 15 million people in the United States.[2] It's also essential to making possible many of the activities that make life worth living: food, leisure, comfort, and travel. Imagine a world without restaurants or hotels. It would be pretty bleak. Travel, tourism, and hospitality, therefore, are vital, not just to the business world, but to our collective well-being.

Hospitality is many things: rigorous and grueling, glamorous and exclusive, maddening, invigorating, inspiring, frustrating, and electrifying. Sometimes you experience all these emotions in the span of a single work day! But one thing it is not is *boring*. By the time you finish this book, I'm confident you'll agree.

1   EHL Insights, "Hospitality industry statistics to have on your radar 2024," Aug. 23, 2024, *https://hospitalityinsights.ehl.edu/hospitality-industry-statistics*

2   U.S. Bureau of Labor Statistics, "Leisure and Hospitality: Workforce Statistics," 2024, *https://www.bls.gov/iag/tgs/iag70.htm#workforce*

CHAPTER 2

WESTWARD AND UPWARD

I t's April 13, 1975, Beirut, Lebanon. On a warm spring Sunday morning, gunmen fire their weapons from a speeding car at Pierre Gemayel and other Lebanese Phalangists as the victims are leaving church. Later that day, a bloody retaliation ensues as the Phalangists massacre two dozen members of a rival group traveling on a bus on a narrow Beirut street.

By the time the sun sets, the fragile peace that kept the fractured nation together is shattered. The Lebanese Civil War has begun.

I was five years old. My family lived in Beirut, not far from the shootings. We were a big family: I had eight siblings and was the second-youngest of the group. My father was in the wholesale food business. My mother was a homemaker who managed to keep our huge household together. She was well dressed, wise, and always found the good in people. For her, it wasn't about the glass being half full or half empty. If the glass had any water in it at all, it was already a blessing!

We had a happy home. But the war convulsed the entire country, and Beirut was the explosive epicenter. No one was unaffected. By the end of 1975, the once-beautiful downtown of the capital, which had long been called the Paris of the Middle East, was reduced to rubble. The city was cleaved in two by the Green Line, which separated the warring Muslim and Christian sides. Despite the boundary, they still found a way to kill each other. The conflict was as complex as it was deadly, involving many factions and driven by various intertwining factors, which dimmed any hope of resolution. It would last fifteen years and claim more than 150,000 lives.

My family endured for five months before my parents decided it was unsafe to remain in Lebanon. My two older brothers were already living in the US. My eldest brother Salem, 22 years my senior, had married an American lady, Beth-Ann, and was now a U.S. citizen. This helped pave the way for our emigration.

So, like many Lebanese at the time, we left our homeland, departing by ship for the Mediterranean island of Cyprus, about 120 miles away. There, we applied for visas at the U.S. Embassy. Several weeks later our applications were approved, and my large family and I were bound for America.

At five I had only a vague understanding of what was going on, or where we were headed. We settled in Atlanta, where my eldest brothers lived, and which had a sizable Lebanese community. That was the first time I ever saw a black guy. I marveled at his dark skin and distinct hair, so different from what I was used to seeing in Lebanon. That was the first of many surprises as we settled into our new home. The fact that my father and siblings spoke English already smoothed our transition.

In 1978, Salem moved to Abu Dhabi to pursue a business opportunity. He worked in the finance department for an oil company. Eventually he expanded into other ventures, opening a dry cleaners, Lebanese restaurants, and the first 7/11 in Abu Dhabi.

In 1982, my parents joined him in the United Arab Emirates, but I remained in America. This made for an unconventional upbringing, as I was raised mostly by my older brothers and sisters, but despite this, I lived the mostly normal life of a typical American kid. In the summers, I'd travel to Abu Dhabi to spend time with family, a joyous occasion, despite the excruciating desert heat.

As I said, my eldest brother Salem was born a couple decades before me, which made him more of a paternal than a fraternal figure. Even though he wasn't around much, he still cast an authoritative shadow over all of us. He was tough on us younger siblings, and that toughness was amplified by the vastly different environments in which we grew up. He was, literally, from another generation, one that was more rigid and traditional, which extolled the value of hard work and the virtue of struggle. He also strove to make us appreciate what our father, a self-made man, had been forced to endure to provide a good life for us.

Salem would visit us in Atlanta every two or three years. His method of whipping us into shape was harsh. He was overly critical, about everything: what I said, how I behaved, how I dressed. I felt like he was always scrutinizing me, waiting to find fault with something, like a

Marine drill sergeant berating a recruit for not shining his shoes properly or making his bed according to the Corps' exacting standards.

By the time I turned 17, a youthful spirit of rebellion was welling inside me. It wasn't just Salem and his watchful eye. I harbored some resentment toward my parents for leaving me back in the U.S. I missed them terribly. Today, I understand that they did it for my own benefit; that I was better off living in the U.S., and they could better provide for the family by working in Abu Dhabi. But at the time, the separation just fueled my angst.

I also, deep down, understood Salem had my best interest at heart—he *had* to be tough on us in order to give us the mental strength, social graces (he was big on teaching etiquette), and the tenacity we needed to survive. But it was sometimes aggravating.

On one of his visits, he called me from the other room.

"Haitham! Come here!"

I trudged into the living room, bracing myself for a tongue lashing.

"Did you leave the lights on?"

And so began a lecture on the importance of frugality and the folly of wasting electricity, concluding with his favorite refrain: ""You don't know how difficult it is to raise nine children! Our father and I are breaking our backs for you!"

And, on this particular point, Salem was right. I shouldn't have left the lights on. But this encounter didn't sit right with me, and I realized, *I don't have to deal with this all the time. I can carve my own way, and then no one can tell me what to do. I wanted independence.*

On that day I vowed to find a way to be independent, to rely on no one, not financially, socially, or emotionally. I wasn't cutting off my family, whom I loved, but I did need to make a change.

I wanted to make my way in the world.

ON MY OWN

At 17, I moved out of the house. What I lacked in financial resources, I made up for in the determination to persevere and make it on my own, with no one's assistance.

That was when I started working as a dishwasher. For the first couple of months I crashed on a friend's couch and scraped together enough money from the job to sign a lease on an apartment. It was hard. Sometimes I didn't have a dollar to my name. I had the power cut off, the phone service suspended, and the landlord chasing me for rent when I fell behind. I resisted the temptation to call my dad or Salem, who would have bailed me out. Instead, I told them: "I'm doing great here."

After high school, I enrolled in college, which amplified the pressure since now I had the expense of higher education, plus the demands of juggling work and school. Sometimes I had to take semester-long breaks just to manage things. But I stuck with it.

I knew no matter what, I couldn't throw in the towel and go back home. I had to make this work. Washing dishes became my lifeline to a brighter future.

Forget what anyone says about washing dishes being "low skill" work. It's not a job you can do lazily while you daydream about your weekend plans—if you slip up, you'll elicit the wrath of the waiters, the cooks, and the chef. Slip up several times and you'll be out on the street, polishing your resume. It might be one of the lowest positions on the hospitality hierarchy, but it takes skill to do it right and assiduous dedication to do it with *excellence.*

There was a learning curve. At first, when I saw dishes piling up, I'd get anxious. Later, I got more relaxed and could organize myself more, and be more methodical in my approach. I learned the "rhythm" of how to do it efficiently and, not simply with speed, but *agility.* After a few days on the job, I was no longer intimidated by the stacks of sticky, oily pots and pans and piles of used silverware, because I knew how to keep pace.

I strove for perfection. Hotels and restaurants are like factory assembly lines: every station on the assembly line plays a vital role. Mistakes or delays at any point cause bottlenecks down the chain. So, if you don't have dishware or bowls ready and the waiter or chef needs to plate the food, your slip-up in the washroom (the proper name for the dishwashing station) affects everything downstream. And the cardinal sin of hospitality is making customers *wait*, whether you're serving a meal or checking them into their room. People hate that.

So, as a dishwasher, even if you never set eyes on the guests dining on Spaghetti Bolognese or tiramisu, your work impacts them.

Besides serving the customers, your job, in a more direct sense, is serving the waiters. Don't make their job tougher. And God forbid you make them look bad by giving them wine glasses with water spots or dinnerware smudged with fingerprints, which will only generate complaints and delays. Waiters have enough stress to deal with without a careless dishwasher adding to it.

All this requires a steadfast attention to detail, which is one of the hallmarks of the industry. Have you ever eaten in a Michelin-starred restaurant? The attention to detail provided by every person who works there will blow your mind. They do things with the artistry of a painter and the precision of a surgeon; things you'd never even think of.

But in the hotel business, that meticulousness is evident not only in the premier establishments of the world, but in any quality place where the employees take pride in their work. Pride and recognition are the real rewards of a hotelier, even more than salary. You can tell a true, professional hotelier from an amateur based on how they respond to recognition. Give them a raise, and sure, they'll be pleased, but present them with an award or certificate of excellence they can put on the wall, they'll be ecstatic.

A good hotelier approaches the work like an artisan approaches their craft: they strive for mastery. And if you want to succeed in *any* field, you must be a master. You must outshine everyone.

Now, dishwashers are, at best, unsung heroes of the kitchen: no one is giving the dishwasher congratulatory plaques or honoring their contributions at black-tie awards ceremonies. But, just because no one is signing your praises, does not mean your craft goes unnoticed. As I said, hospitality folks are an alert bunch; they pick up on the details; they're attuned to a hundred things; they're skilled at filtering out the "noise" and observing what matters.

And if you come in every day and night, striving to be the best damn dishwasher you can be, you will be noticed.

That's how I was able to create new avenues for myself.

As I got more experienced and felt like I had things under control, even during busy hours, I'd venture out from the washroom into the kitchen, take mental notes and observe the chefs in their element.

The chef, sweating over the stove, would see me watching and say, "Haitham, what the hell are you doing standing around? Go check on the baked potatoes!" Or "Haitham, go check on the bacon!"

I'd run over and report back: "Chef, the bacon's ready!"

"Take it out and bring it over here! Goddamn it, hurry up!"

I'd watch and see how he'd lay the bacon trays, and then take the initiative to do it for him next time. I didn't wait for people to tell me what to do—as a dishwasher, none of this was even part of my job description—but I learned by observation, stepped up, and made myself useful.

So, when the chef said, "Oh shit, I forgot to put in the bacon," I'd be able to say, "Don't worry, I got it."

Gradually, I became more familiar with the myriad activities going on behind the kitchen line, studying other team members and understanding how a restaurant kitchen works, until the chef barked more orders.

"Take these dishes, start to garnish, drop some wings in the fryer, take out the broccoli!" The more I became available to the chef, the more he called on me to pitch in. And, once I observed a given task a couple times, I could do it, making sure to stay one step ahead of the chef every time. So, by the time he asked, I was already doing it, or had it finished.

Next, I learned to read the orders. As the chef would grumble about one thing or another, I'd peer at the tickets over his shoulder and jump in.

"Chef, I got your wings down for 46!"

"Okay, good. Put some cheese sticks on there as well... and I need some fries!"

I'd help his team whenever there was chaos. That's how I learned how to cook. Did I make mistakes? Sure. I'd over-cook the bacon or fry the wings to a crisp, but usually I only made these mistakes *once*. After that, I got it.

That was the genesis of my talent for multitasking at pace, one of the cornerstones of my professional life. Today, I'm working at the executive level, but the foundational skills that have made me an asset at the upper echelon of the company, I acquired in the trenches of the kitchen. Now, people can trust me to juggle half a dozen things. I suppose, for me, it's a combination of innate ability with practiced skill. Most people are poor at multitasking. But if you can multitask effectively and fast, you're well positioned for success in this industry.

Multitasking is closely intertwined with *timing,* an art unto itself. If you're tackling multiple tasks at once, you must be efficient and tactical in understanding what gets done when.

Timing was one of the biggest things I learned from chefs. If you have a multiple-item order, everything must be ready to be served at the same time. If the customer has ordered eggs with a side of hashbrowns, plus mushrooms, and avocado toast, what goes on the fire first? Figuring this out demands precision, foresight, and a methodical approach to work.

In a sense, getting a single breakfast order right is a microcosm of the hotel operation as a whole: a defined process based on coordination, agility, timing, and efficiency.

Even today, when I cook at home, I have five people to feed. I want all the plates to look the same and come out at the same time.

I've adapted this approach to my corporate work too, and it offers an important lesson for any white-collar worker, regardless of their industry. Procrastinators look at big items and leave them to the end, preferring to tick off the small things first. But the big tasks just roll over to the next day, and the next, and the next, and pretty soon you're scrambling to meet a deadline. And because it's the complex assignment you've left to the last minute, you'll probably make mistakes.

That's another habit of mine: tackle the big stuff early in the morning. The stuff you hate doing. I know my energy peaks in the morning, so I harness that power to knock off the more taxing tasks. And then, at the end of the day, when my energy is spent, I can complete those smaller to-dos. Initially, I wasn't like that at all, but, with time, I trained myself through trial and error, developing a system that worked.

I learned that from cooking: get the big stuff done first.

RISING THROUGH THE RANKS

Owing to my self-imposed apprenticeship in the kitchen, I managed to get promoted to breakfast cook at age 18. After that, I wanted to learn how to bartend and wait tables, so I tackled it in much the same way: shadowing, learning, understanding the "systems" and processes that made everything function. Stepping up and volunteering to help the waitstaff, bartenders, and kitchen staff whenever possible. No one was going to volunteer to train me (they were busy with their own stuff), but by volunteering to fill gaps, I became someone they could rely on. As a result, I was given more responsibility and embraced as a key part of the team.

I'm an introvert by nature, so waiting tables trained me in being an extravert. I put all my heart into it. I always wanted to do the best. To outshine everyone. No task was too small for improvement or optimization. If another waiter would serve dinner in 20 minutes, I'd try to do it in 15. If it took the average person two weeks to learn something, I'd have to attempt to master it in one. It was all about efficiency for me.

I did envy people who were ahead of me career-wise. Comparison is, as they say, the thief of joy, but a little bit of covetousness is a great motivator. I wanted to be stronger, better, faster. My mother used to give me that advice in my school days: "be a bit envious of those who are top of your class, watch what they do, and try to do the same or better. This is how people grow," she said.

In my zeal to be the best, I did err. I'd step on people's feet, or crash into waiters while bussing tables. Sometimes, my own ambition got the best of me and I made enemies rather than friends. But I course-corrected, pulled back, recalibrated. Those who cared about me gave me feedback, and I corrected my words and actions.

Through it all, I was driven by a strong sense of purpose: I wanted to prove to everyone I could do it. To prove it to *myself*, above all, that not only could I survive living on my own, but that I could *thrive and be the best version of myself.*

Working toward a purpose is different than simply waiting tables to get by, and pay the bills.

And good thing I had that motivation. I learned early on in my adventure of independent living that one job wasn't going to cut it, so I held down two, and sometimes three jobs at the same time.

On the weekends, I waited tables at Maximilian's. Maximilian's was a storied restaurant in Marietta, Georgia, with white tablecloths, an exclusive clientele, and exquisite dishes like grilled salmon filet, table-side prepared Caesar salad, and caramelized banana flambé. But the place had a checkered past. A historic 19th century home, it was the first in the city with a swimming pool. At one point, it was owned by a political official (a local mayor, I believe), but the luxurious addition of the pool became a curse when the mayor's son drowned. Their dream home had become a nightmare, and the bereaved family sold it. It passed through various hands and, eventually, became a restaurant.

The house did look pretty creepy. It was in the middle of a forest, and every waiter, cook, and busboy had a story about some encounter with supernatural forces, presumably the ghost of the drowned son. Spooky phenomena like lights flickering and doors banging. These stories, passed down by restaurant staff to wide-eyed employees, new on the job, became part of the lore of Maximilian's.

As for me, the scariest thing I experienced there was an overcooked steak.

Despite the rumored presence of spirits (the ghostly kind, not the liquid kind—that was in abundance), it was an enviable place to work. Guests were charged 20% gratuity, so I used to take home around $80-100 a night waiting tables for just six hours. That's $300 extra a week for a weekend's worth of shifts, which was great money in the early '90s, especially considering that was supplementing my regular paycheck from the hotel.

Anyway, a 20% tip could be a little or a lot, depending on the size of the party. You could really cash in when you waited on big groups, but that required a higher skill level I didn't yet have.

One of our veteran waiters was a guy called Larry, or LB. Larry had long hair, a style that wasn't permitted for men, so, during shifts, he had to wear a wig, which he affectionately called Lisa. He was twice my age but had the vivacity and good humor of a 20-year-old.

One rainy afternoon I arrived for my shift. The place hadn't opened yet; we were doing our prep work (which in LB's case meant prepping Lisa).

As I washed the lettuce, still fresh and fragrant from the Georgia farm where it was sourced, LB gave me some professional advice.

"Haitham, the money is in the groups. If you wanna get anywhere, you gotta work those big tables."

I said I wasn't ready yet.

"Stick with me. I'll teach you what you need to know," he offered.

He really did teach me everything about the job, all the little tricks and nuances that only come with experience and, given that he had been doing this for a couple decades, he knew every trick in the book. It was definitely his calling—he lived a comfortable lifestyle from it and desired no other station.

Larry honed my skills in multitasking and timing. For example, imagine the customer has ordered a baked potato, a steak, and a salad. How do you prep them so they're all ready at once? At Maximilian's, waiters handled the cold foods. Salads, for example: you have to dress and plate them yourself. If you have salmon with that salad, the chef needs to know the salmon is coming too, so he can put it on the fire.

Under Larry's mentorship, my waiting skills improved significantly. But I was still hesitant about serving big groups.

One night we had a reservation for 26.

Larry said, "You're gonna take that table."

"I can't do it," I said. At that time, the biggest table I had waited was six.

"Yes, you can. I got your back."

When the doors opened, I was nervous—but the good kind of nervous. When you know you're being tested and you're eager to prove to yourself you can do it.

He advised me: remember orders, don't let your mind wander, stay focused.

The massive party arrived. One tipsy lady, probably five cocktails deep already, eyed me up and down and said, "He looks just like my ex-husband John!"

Great, I thought, *what an unlucky start.* But her friends had a laugh, and that broke the tension. I laughed with them, and decided then and there that the best way to approach this challenge was to have fun with it. They all called me John for the rest of the dinner.

That evening, LB followed through on his promise, backing me up, making sure I remembered the order, taking care to point out any oversights in case I forgot something. He reminded me to take out the bread basket and the butter, and helped make sure all the dishes were ready to be served at the same time. One of the essential tasks of a waiter and not the sole responsibility of the chef, as one might think.

Things were going well. We'd made it through the round of appetizers, main courses, several rounds of drinks, largely without a hitch, but the kitchen was slow with a couple of guests' baked salmon. This is another skill that separates a pro waiter from an amateur; if something is late, you must keep your customers entertained and distracted. Be candid about the delay while maintaining an air of professionalism and total control. I made small talk while LB went to the kitchen to help speed things up. I breathed a sigh of relief when he came back through the double doors with a steaming plate of salmon in each hand, roasted to perfection.

It was a small victory, but it boosted my confidence. I was grateful to Larry for ushering me through it, and for giving me the table in the first place. I banked nearly three hundred bucks just from tips from that table, so it was like he had given me that money from his own pocket. He was that kind of guy: selfless, generous, a true team player.

I often wonder how he's doing now. He would be in his eighties, probably happily retired and fishing somewhere. Though, knowing LB, I wouldn't be surprised if he was still waiting tables somewhere, showing some young buck how it's done.

THE NEXT CHALLENGE

While things were going well at Maximilian's, back at the Marriott, I was also distinguishing myself as a waiter, and soon they bumped me up to restaurant supervisor. I had really found my groove there. Our team was good at our jobs, but we didn't let our professionalism get in the way of having fun. Even now, I can picture the faces of that zany cast of characters as if they were sitting here with me in my 22nd floor office in Dubai.

Cody, a young African-American guy who worked as a breakfast cook, was best known around the place for perpetual tardiness. Every morning, shortly after (sometimes *long* after) the 5:00am start time, there was Cody, barging through the swinging double doors into the kitchen like a tornado, tying his apron and throwing on his hat as he scrambled to get the oven on and do his prep work.

Cody had an infectious sense of humor and loved to take the mickey out of the waitresses. He was a consummate party animal, a big reason, I suppose, for his frequent lateness. The first hour of his shift was always chaos, but once he warmed up and fell into a rhythm, he'd scramble those eggs, fry that bacon, and cook those pancakes with aplomb.

Then there was Beth, a lady with Down's syndrome who was super funny, with a wit and comic timing as sharp as anyone. But as soon as the kitchen got busy, she swapped her jocular attitude for a more serious demeanor, rolled up her sleeves, and got to work.

Carlos was a dishwasher from Mexico who spoke not one word of English. Trying to communicate with Carlos was an adventure in itself. We'd employ a combination of gestures, pidgin English, and rudimentary Spanish (the few words that we knew from kitchen work) until, finally, his face would light up.

"Me no care-o," he'd say—*I don't care.* Then he'd just go back to whatever it was he was doing.

Then there was Dwain, the soporific security guard who was always trying to grab forty winks on shift. It was almost a game: he'd find a new corner of the building to nap in, and we'd try to catch him. Once the fire alarm went off and he slept through it.

For some of them, it was part-time work. For others, it was a full-time job or a career. A real mix of people from different walks of life, who all came together each day and night to make the hotel and restaurant run. That was the common thread: the *shift*. That's when you unite as a unit. Then the shift ends, and everyone goes home, back to their private lives.

While I relished being restaurant supervisor, I already had my eyes on the next prize: restaurant manager. It was a long shot. I was a teenager, barely out of high school. It was unheard of for someone so young to get that role, and besides, there were no openings; the current manager pretty much had the job on lock.

But then a bottle of gin intervened on my behalf.

One day, I showed up at the start of my shift, and the manager was nowhere to be seen. "Have you seen Lisa?" I asked the bartender. (Lisa being the manager, not LB's wig! No relation.)

"Nope," said the bartender.

Lisa rolled in twenty minutes late and reeking of booze. I don't mean just three-martini lunch tipsy; she was out of it, in no state to manage a restaurant. I took her keys and called a taxi to take her home.

The next morning, the general manager called me into his office, after reading the log book, and asked for a debrief. I reported what had happened. "She didn't argue with you when you sent her away?" he asked. "No," I said "she was barely even coherent."

A few days later, management let her go. I didn't know it at the time, but, evidently, it wasn't the first such incident.

They posted the restaurant manager job. Less than a week later the GM said, "Haitham, are you gonna apply?'

"No," I said.

"Why not?"

"Should I?"

"Of course."

Apparently, HR did not have the same confidence in me as my general manager because when I went to their office to ask for an application form, they laughed. I guess they were used to 19-year-olds bussing tables and washing dishes, not gunning for supervisory roles.

Nevertheless, I left the office clutching the form. That night, in my apartment, I filled it out.

A couple weeks later, I officially got the job. That made me the youngest restaurant manager in the history of that hotel. It was a victory that vindicated some of the struggle and sacrifice I had made over the last couple years since I decided to leave home.

In truth, it had been a difficult, stressful period. I was succeeding now, but, during the first year or two, I fell on my face many times. It was a period of trial and error. That's how you learn. It's okay to mess up – as long as you don't repeat your errors. Don't be a habitual offender.

Most of my colleagues at work who were older than me didn't think I would make it. "He won't last a month," they said.

If coming of age means learning to stand on your own two feet, then my decision to set off on my own, and the budding restaurant career I had put together from scratch, certainly helped me grow up from a boy into a man. Independence also shaped me differently from my brothers and sisters, who didn't leave home so early and remained reliant on my parents longer than I had. Later, my father, may he rest in peace, said something that filled me with pride. "Haitham gave me the least amount of trouble!"

As Frank Sinatra, whose tunes I sometimes listened to on my tape deck to and from work, sung, "I did it my way!"

CHAPTER 3

IN THE NOT-SO STILL
OF THE NIGHT

It's 3:00am in downtown Atlanta. The city sleeps. The lobby is still. The guests dream. A businessman or two stagger in after carousing in the bars in Buckhead. The security guards make their rounds. Things are quiet.

But the night manager does not rest. The front office—reception, in layman's terms—is still a hive of activity, as busy as the day shift, just in a different way.

That's where I found myself after a year of working as restaurant manager. During that time, I got exposure to the ins and outs of front office work, and I was promoted into the role. It presented me with an altogether new set of tasks and challenges.

Often, I was on duty overnight, starting at midnight. There was something exciting about working the graveyard shift. There wasn't the buzz of the daylight hours, with people coming and going all the time (though of course there are always late check-ins and early check-outs) but the job was no less demanding or important.

For one, you're the steward of the hotel, responsible for everyone's safety. No matter where you are in the world, crime and chaos tend to occur after the sun goes down. Not to say we dealt with that a lot at the Marriott, but you have to be vigilant. That means overseeing the security team patrolling the property, making sure CCTVs are in working order, and keeping an eye out for any suspicious activity.

Kind of like the lookout on a sailing ship who climbs the "eagle's nest" and gazes out to the dark sea, alert to any hazards in the ship's path. He's the first line of defense. The crew and passengers on the ship depend on him.

Besides keeping general order, the big task was the night audit, which closes out the day and sets the hotel up for the next day. At midnight, when your shift begins, you start running financial reports, processing payments and transactions, and tallying up debits and credits for the rooms, the bar, the restaurant, and other areas. A hotel of this caliber would generate maybe $60,000 a day, roughly 80% of that from rooms. Food and beverage (F&B) is a big money-maker, but also represents the biggest "profit leak" because of high operational costs and lower profit margins (something that affects the restaurant industry broadly, not just hotels). Generally, room revenue compensates for shortfall from bars and restaurants.

Bill was a colleague of mine who loved the graveyard shift. A pro at the night audit, he helped train me when I came on. One night when I was training with Bill, a drunk couple walked in and asked for a room for the night. We were nearly full, but there were one or two unoccupied rooms. When a guest shows up without a reservation, it can take some time to allocate a room and handle their check-in. They started to shout at him because they didn't want to wait.

When the guy's credit card got rejected, Bill and I got the surprise of our lives. He totally lost it and pulled out a gun. "Are you taking me for a ride? Are you trying to embarrass me in front of my lady?" he shouted as he waved the pistol in Bill's face. Bill stayed calm and just reassured the maniac that he was doing his best to accommodate him, respectfully apologizing for the delay at the same time.

"Do I have your permission to run the card again?" asked Bill.

"Fine. But hurry up with it." He was still waving the gun about. I wondered if the thing was loaded. I was operating on the assumption it was.

To my horror, the card was declined again. This wasn't going to end well.

"Amazing, it worked this time!" said Bill, bluffing. He handed the drunkard the room key, and, once he and the woman had stumbled out of the lobby, Bill called the cops, who showed up in a hurry. Minutes later, they led the irate guest out in handcuffs.

Obviously, that's not a common scenario, but it was a dramatic lesson in the random challenges you deal with at reception, and how you sometimes have to think on your feet.

In the front office I applied the same approach that helped me excel as a dishwasher, a bartender, and a waiter—strive for perfection, optimize inefficient processes by cutting unnecessary steps, master multitasking, and make yourself useful even in areas where you're not expected to contribute. Quickly, I learned the ropes. After the first time

I handled the night audit by myself, the general manager came in the next day and asked Bill, "How did Haitham do?"

"This guy's like a sponge!" Bill said.

It wasn't a large hotel, 220 rooms and suites, with one lobby bar and an all-day dining restaurant, so the employees were a tight-knit group. And you really get to know people from working alongside them. You observe their strengths, their shortcomings, and their quirks.

That was, and remains, one of the things I like best about hospitality. It's a people-oriented business. Even as digital technology and automation reinvents some basic functions of the hotel, replacing actual workers with screens and apps, at the end of the day, the essence of hotel or restaurant work is *people serving people*. The human element.

This was pre-mobile phones, so you only had each other for entertainment. There was a landline which was not available for personal calls, so, for all intents and purposes, when you were there, you had no access to the outside world besides a pay phone which was only available on breaks.

So, during break time you were "forced" to be together. It was fun. We'd joke, share gossip, enjoy a meal together, or sit around watching Atlanta Falcons games.

If you had to work holidays or on weekends – when hotels are busiest – your shift workers become your friends and family. When everyone else is at home with their families, you might be eating Christmas pie or carving the Thanksgiving turkey with each other. You just got on with it. It was fun.

It encouraged a camaraderie and intimacy that you find less often now in hotels, an *esprit de corps,* which is perhaps lost forever. These days, laughing and joking together in the break room has been replaced by individual employees hunched over their cellphones, ensconced in their own bubbles. It's regrettable, and I wonder if today's young workers could ever grasp how things used to be.

FRONT AND CENTER

The front office is the nerve center. Everything revolves around it. That was a big change from the restaurant, which is kind of its own self-contained entity.

I loved being in the thick of things at such an operationally important point. I relished the exposure to the constant influx and outflow of guests—mostly businesspeople, but also families, solo travelers, camera-toting tourists—and having that direct, client-facing interaction.

Working at the Courtyard remains a special memory for me. It was a small hotel with one restaurant and a lobby bar, both open to the reception area. Standing behind reception, you practically have a full view of the whole restaurant and lobby bar.

When you arrived for the 6:00am shift, the housekeeping team would still be polishing the marble floors across the entire area. The fresh smell of polish mingled with the savory aromas of sizzling sausage and hash browns coming from the kitchen and breakfast buffet. The dimmed lobby lights from the night shift would be at their brightest by then and you start to hear people's suitcases rolling across the lobby floor on their way to check out. I'll never forget the sensory interplay of sights, smells, and sounds: the hotel coming alive for another day.

I learned how much work goes into taking a booking, blocking the room, checking in, and checking out. It requires a lot of coordination and synchronization between different parts of the hotel, especially housekeeping. This synchronization is testament to the elegantly "mechanical" nature of a hotel, which, like a vast and complex machine, requires all the moving parts to work in harmony for the whole structure to run.

Most guests are unaware of this: they check in, drop their bags, dine in the restaurant, lounge in the lobby, sleep, and check out. They take for granted that the room they reserved will be available, that housekeeping will replace towels when they needed, and that breakfast will be hot and available on time. In a well-run hotel, this all happens seamlessly, so guests don't give what goes on "behind the scenes" a second thought. But that seamlessness requires a high degree of professionalism, efficiency, and coordination.

Back then, there were no online reservations, which must seem antiquated to younger people accustomed to booking a room anywhere in the world with just a few taps on a smartphone. You would call it in or fax it, or people would book through travel agents who had access to the computerized network (primitive compared to the high-tech networks used today) known as the "global distribution system."

In the restaurant, your work tends to be confined to the restaurant. But the front office interfaces with multiple departments to manage things effectively: housekeeping, engineering, laundry, etc. These are "remote" tasks, done out of sight and reach of the front desk. And it all has to be efficient. If you're working reception, it's almost like you're a commander in war responsible for managing your troops, deployed in various units all over the front lines. You have to know who is doing what at any giving moment and make sure all units are working in sync, especially during busy hours when there's a mad dash of incoming and outgoing guests.

Those were the days of landlines and walkie talkies. Later, the biggest tech innovation of the '90s was that a housekeeper could register a room as being cleaned via a portable, smartphone-like device. Now, even that seems primitive. Today's technology has made communication and integration between the front office and other departments easier and instantaneous.

Technology hasn't fixed everything. Yet! One of the cardinal customer service sins in our business is making people wait. It's a scientific fact—really, check the studies—that human beings find waiting in line maddening, unless you're British! And, whether traveling for business or pleasure, it's the last thing you want to do after a long journey or before departing for a stressful day of air travel.

DON'T MAKE ANYONE WAIT!

At the Courtyard, we were excellent at minimizing wait time for check-ins or check-outs, and this was in the late '80s, without the benefit of digitized systems and complex software to coordinate the moving parts.

Thirty-five years later, some hotels, even high-end ones, are still trying to figure that out. Recently I visited one of our hotels where I saw people standing in line. I called the GM down and said, "See that line? That's not luxury. We have to do better."

When you reserve a room, you get an automatic email confirmation which asks for your arrival details (time, flight number, etc.). People on the morning shift pull up that list, as well as a list of departures. You marry the leaving list with the departure list and cross-reference who is coming and going. At busier hotels, you have near 100% occupancy, so there is little margin for error.

And in luxury establishments, you have to harmonize room availability with individual client requests, such as a regular who doesn't want a room near the elevators, or demands a suite with a view of the river, but not the city. This only works if you talk to people and find out what they really need and want. Sometimes that just means asking, "Sorry, the room is not ready. What can I do to make you happy?" Perhaps they just need a place to shower or a quiet space to take a business call, and that's enough to assuage their concerns.

It requires a lot of human attention; even today, not all of it is automated. You need humans to *plan* ahead of time. Again, this is where multitasking comes into play: juggling many balls in your head at once. And the art of paying close attention to detail.

At the Courtyard Marriott, we used Excel sheets to manage all this stuff. Excel debuted in 1985, so it was still kind of cutting-edge by the early '90s. Now every office worker in the world knows Excel; back then, when personal computing was a rarity, it was a novelty.

SHADOWING SALES

Since my first moments plunging my arms into tubs of scalding water to scrub sticky pots and oily pans, I wanted to be proficient in every facet of the hospitality business. Following my initiation, I had become familiar with bartending, waiting tables, rooms, and other operations, and now, of course, front office work. I had always pushed myself to master every role, no matter how unglamorous.

But there was one area of the business that I hadn't cracked. One that held a special allure: sales and marketing.

Picking up on my earlier metaphor, if the hotel is like a military deployment, the sales team are special ops. They dressed sharply, drove expensive cars, walked with a swagger and confidence, and often traveled off-site for "secret missions"—okay, just client visits, but still, there was something cool about what they did. They seemed more like entrepreneurs than nine to five employees, and there is of course some truth to that. In a corporate sales role: you work for the company, but you're also responsible for building your own Rolodex (another tool of the trade that has gone the way of the landline!)

Anyway, I asked if I could shadow the team. Since it was a small hotel, there were just three people in the sales department, headed by Amy, a veteran who had been with Marriott for many years. She generated the most revenue for the hotel through corporate clients (rooms, meetings, events, group stays). I was fascinated. How did she get there? What were the secrets to selling? Why did she outshine the others?

She shared a lot of wisdom, as well as the ups and downs of the role. She told me candidly that, while she loved her job, there were days when the stress was unbearable. The sales team faced high expectations to keep a steady stream of clients walking through the front door. When business faltered, everyone immediately pointed fingers at sales. Competition with other hotels was intense, and you had to roll with the seasonal fluctuations of the market. The low seasons really forced you, she said, to be on top of your game as you had to work twice as hard to keep your numbers up.

I went with her on client visits a few times, where I studied her comportment: friendly, chatty, maintaining good rapport. She knew their families and what was going on in their lives. Amy was a friend they trusted. It taught me a key lesson: sales often has little to do with selling at all.

Observing Amy also helped me hone one of my own superpowers, which I mentioned has aided me at every step of my career—relationship building. All business is people-centric, but in hospitality, it's on another level. And just like most fields, the higher you ascend, the smaller that world gets. Even in a *global* industry. By that I mean, when you climb the hierarchy high enough, the air is thinner and there are few others at your level. So, opportunities for advancement are slim and reputation is *everything*. Consequently, friends you make in, say, New York City in 2024 might open doors for you in Moscow in 2030. It goes the other way too—get on someone's bad side, and they could become your enemy later on.

The other two salespeople in the department couldn't just count on legacy accounts; they had to work a lot harder to thrive. One was a recent hire who came on with just a few clients and really had to hustle to earn his keep. Sales is a competitive role that takes time to bear fruit.

He felt pressured to lower prices to win new business. But this strategy wasn't ideal because once you bring someone in at a low price, it's difficult to raise prices later. You end up painting yourself into a corner.

With time and experience, you learn the nuances of the relationship between pricing, value, and loyalty. As any veteran salesman will tell you, undercutting on price is rarely the best way to convince clients to work with you.

Ever the sponge, I absorbed these lessons with great interest, and quietly contemplated the possibility that, one day, I would find a home in the sales department somewhere.

NEW FRONTIERS

Now in my early twenties, I had acquired a depth and breadth of experience and a strong foothold in both the industry and within the Marriott system. It was time to jump to the next rung of the ladder.

Today, Marriott is the largest hotel chain in the world by number of rooms—1.6 million in 139 countries; not bad for a company that started as a single root beer stand in DC in 1927. In the '80s it was not quite as big but still a giant, one of the major chains. That meant ample opportunity for internal promotion.

I aspired to work at a bigger hotel and be exposed to fresh opportunities and challenges that would sharpen my skillset. A spot for a receptionist opened up in the front office of the Marriott Marquis, a 1600-room complex in downtown Atlanta. I applied and was accepted.

This was like a baseball player with a single-A minor league club in a sleepy town getting called up to play AAA ball in a mid-sized city. I wasn't quite in the major leagues yet, but it was definitely a step up. Everything suddenly got bigger, faster, and more intense. The Courtyard Marriott housed, at most, 250 guests. In the Marquis a typical day involved 800 people checking in and 1,200 checking out, or vice-versa. You might be serving *two thousand* people at breakfast. While before, we hosted small corporate gatherings of a dozen or so folks, now we had to manage 1,000-person conventions and huge, lavish weddings.

My fellow receptionists and I competed to have the best check-in speed. Speed is key, but not at the expense of quality or making any mistakes at check-in. I soon learned that speed operates in tandem with efficiency and agility.

A botched check-in causes disasters. And we had our share during busy times when we were stretched to the limit. Check in a guest to a dirty room because you overlooked that it had not yet been "released" by housekeeping or even worse, check in someone into an occupied room, and you're going to have one, if not several, irate customers chirping at you to fix it! And believe me, with even more advanced technology at hotels today, such errors still occur.

Working in such a big hotel was an incredible experience. It was amazing how such a huge machine could operate day in day out.

The new role also sharpened my people skills, and my acumen for remembering names, faces, professions, preferences, and quirks. Especially with repeat guests' preferences. From a particular room they liked, to whether they were an early riser or a night owl, to dietary restrictions and a whole range of other things. All the stuff that makes the difference between a satisfied guest and another entry in the complaint book.

Often, it wasn't a matter of fulfilling requests, but simply spotting a familiar face. When guests return to a hotel and the concierge recognizes them and greets them by name, it makes a difference. People love to be welcomed back. It makes them feel at home. I think that if a hotel can give people the feeling of *home*, even though they're thousands of miles from friends, family and everything they know, we've succeeded.

In the late 90's, we worked on a lodging system called Opera, which had a feature called the Guest Profile, which tracked not just basic data like dates of past stays but personal preferences in room amenities, food, etc. We strove to cater to these idiosyncrasies. This is how we made everyone feel recognized and appreciated for their patronage. It's how we made them feel special.

Today, technological advances provide us a hundred ways to record and deliver guest preferences, down to the most granular detail. But as powerful and efficient as those systems are, sometimes the technology actually becomes counterproductive. Why? Because relying too much on digital systems can feel "robotic" and sap the experience of the human touch, which ultimately is what matters.

DESTINATION WEDDING

Even while juggling several jobs and pursuing a college degree, I carved out time every summer to visit my family in Abu Dhabi. It was always a joyous occasion when the plane touched down and I was embraced by a dozen relatives—brothers, sisters, cousins, and, of course, my parents.

In addition to family members, I spent time with a small social circle of friends and acquaintances: locals who didn't travel abroad during the scorching summers, Emirati students who studied overseas but returned during the break, and other people like me who had family in Abu Dhabi. One evening, at a group dinner, a friend of mine invited her cousin, a woman six years my junior named Zeina, a name that means "beauty" in Arabic. Zeina and I were seated next to each other and hit it off immediately. She was fun, chatty, inquisitive, and bright, and I knew I wanted to see her again.

Things quickly progressed from friendship to romance, and we were married within the year, in Abu Dhabi.

By that point, I had moved from Atlanta to Orlando, where my brothers and sisters relocated to years prior. Zeina applied for permission to join me in the States, and, once granted, she lived with me in Florida. It was a tough year for two newlyweds, surviving on a single income and one car in a place where public transit is virtually non-existent. But we made it work.

I was working in the front office in a Marriott hotel, and while the responsibilities were mostly the same as before, the clientele was not. In Atlanta we catered chiefly to business travelers, but in Orlando we served domestic and international tourists visiting for leisure. These guests had different needs. They tend to be pickier because, unlike the corporates, they're paying out of their own pocket. And, because leisure travelers tend to spend more time in the hotel, every detail becomes critical. Generally, they're harder to please when it comes to food, cleaning and housekeeping.

I learned a lot about people and cultures there. Which was useful training for the next phase of my career, which would (little did I know at the time) take me far beyond the borders of the United States.

In one unforgettable incident, an elderly couple from the UK experienced the worst thing that can happen when you're on an international holiday: death. The husband passed away in his sleep. His wife found his body in the morning.

She came down to reception, distraught, and pleaded frantically, "My husband isn't waking up!" I don't think she could even bear to verbalize the awful truth she must have already known: *my husband is dead.*

We called an ambulance, but there was no chance of reviving the man. When something like this happens in a foreign country, your grief is compounded by major logistical and legal complications: you have to make a million calls and fill out a lot of paperwork to repatriate the body. Their kids flew in from the UK to help, but the whole affair was a disaster. It was devastating to see this elderly lady having to go through such trauma so far from home. What really struck me was the *despair* that she so clearly felt. Until the moment your loved one's last breath leaves their body, you can still hope, no matter how ill they might be. But that moment of finality, that moment of everything coming to an end, is difficult to comprehend or contemplate.

Hotels are people's home away from home. And no one likes to think about it when they're traveling, but tragedies that occur at home can also happen far away. In hospitality, we provide a means for customers to enjoy their highest highs—a wedding, giving the keynote speech at a major convention, a once-in-a-lifetime vacation, a career-making business meeting where a major deal is signed—but also, sometimes, their lowest lows. As a hotelier, especially in a client-facing front office role, you must be prepared to navigate both.

If there was a silver lining to this tale, it was seeing the woman embraced by her children, who left the UK on the first flight they could catch to be with her. In her moment of grief, she was supported and loved. It was deeply touching, and, as I observed the scene from behind the check-in desk, it reminded me that family is everything, no matter what distance separates you. My parents had left Lebanon to give us a better life in America, then changed countries again to pursue opportunities they didn't have in the States. I missed my mother and father, who were getting on in years. Moreover, my mother's health was in decline.

I started to think: is it time for me to go back east and rejoin them?

I wrestled with the decision for a long time. America was really the only home I had ever known. Where would I live? Where would I work? What was the work culture like there? What kind of lifestyle would I have?

One condition for returning was that I'd only work for a big international brand which I knew would have SOPs (Standard Operating Procedures) that were, at least, familiar. I didn't want to have to learn an entirely new way of doing business from scratch.

After much rumination, I decided to make the move. But I didn't want to go before locking down a job.

I perused the employment listings in the region, which were scant. But then my eyes landed on one notice for a role in the front office of InterContinental's hotel in Dubai. InterContinental has a sparkling reputation. I didn't know anything about that particular hotel, but I threw my hat in. Soon, I got a call back: they were interested. The guy who took me through the hiring process was named Antoine, a fellow Lebanese American. He put to rest a lot of my concerns. I did well in the job interviews—all conducted over the phone—and they extended me an offer.

Suddenly, it all became real. It was coming together. Soon I would be leaving behind the life I knew, trading the old for something altogether new. Such moments are both nerve-racking and exhilarating. But they're also the "pivots" where the most growth happens.

At the end of my last night shift at the Orlando Marriott, I went up to the roof at daybreak. The sun was rising in the east—somewhere out there, tens of thousands of miles away, my family, and my new life, waited. *Let's see what the future has to offer,* I thought.

It was time.

CHAPTER 4

FORTUNE FAVORS
THE FEARLESS

In Dubai, every five-star hotel boasts at least one world-class restaurant, where creative, eye-popping dishes are prepared by award-winning chefs. But unlike such meals, career opportunity is rarely served up by a white-gloved waiter on a silver platter. Instead, you have to go out and find such opportunities for yourself.

In my case, I had to hustle my way into the world of five-star hospitality. After working my way up the ladder from dishwasher to the front office, I now had my sights set on sales and marketing, even though I had no experience in that department. But the thing about this industry is that, no matter where you find yourself, there is always a chance to move, grow, or advance, if you're willing to work for it.

When I made the leap to Dubai, my parents were living in Abu Dhabi, the UAE capital. My mother, who was ill with heart disease, had always wanted me to work closer to them. In truth, I wasn't sure how much more time she had. Her health would deteriorate and then just as quickly she'd bounce back, only to fall ill again. She was literally in and out of the hospital every other week. Yet she was resilient, patient, and had faith. She believed strongly in God's will, and her positive energy filled the hearts of her family.

On weekends, I would drive to Abu Dhabi to stay with my parents. That time meant the world to them and to me. One weekend, I had just picked up my mother from a three-day hospital stay. She was feeling better and the doctors gave her permission to go home.

"Haitham, I feel like some ice cream," she said. I went out to oblige her request and sat with her as she enjoyed her scoop of rose, pistachio, and Arabic gum-flavored milk ice cream. After, my father, mother, and I sat and chatted. She was glowing with happiness as we laughed together, and my father and I teased her about a certain beanie she was wearing on her head.

The conversation flowed until my mother decided she was going to go to bed early. I promised her that I would go out with her the next morning to buy her a new dress, and we said goodnight.

As she walked away from us toward her bedroom, she dropped the beanie off her head. She reached down to pick it up, and I rushed to pick it up for her so she wouldn't have to kneel down. As I handed it back to her, we looked at each other and she smiled at me.

Little did I know, that was the last time I would lock eyes with her and see her beautiful smile. She went to bed, and never woke up again.

It was a devastating emotional blow. I would never feel the soft embrace of my mother again, nor hear her infectious laugh.

After she passed, I questioned whether I wanted to stay in Dubai at all. But my dad was still around, and he was heartbroken. I wanted to be there for him. He and my mother had been married for over 50 years.

Despite my grief, I did my best to focus on work. And there was much to do. At the time, my hotel was trading below its market share. The competition had edged us out.

I was working at the prestigious InterContinental Hotel as the front office manager. This was a legacy hotel: opened in 1975, it was the first five-star hotel and the first major international establishment to open in Dubai. It was renowned for its restaurants and the rooftop bar, Up on the Tenth, which boasted beautiful views across the water. With guests from all over the world coming and going, it was a lively place.

My new position came with more responsibility than I had before. Now, I was in charge of overseeing the reception, bellstaff, concierge, transportation, guest relations, and the club lounge, among other functions. Not to mention it was a much bigger and busier hotel, as well. It was great exposure to different facets of the business.

I found an apartment for rent within walking distance of the hotel, although I quickly learned that walking was only possible when it was cooler outside. With temperatures often skyrocketing to 40°C (104°F) and above, I had to drive, which, ironically, took *longer* than walking due to traffic, parking, and waiting for the air conditioning to kick in to cool the car down.

Dubai was radically different from the environment I had grown up in. Back then, it was not the gleaming, glamorous metropolis it is today; it was more desert than city. There were camel crossings across the two-lane highway.

Sandstorms would blow through, leaving behind beige-colored mounds of sand that blocked roads throughout the city. Not to mention the stray camels that would suddenly decide to cross the road, causing deadly accidents.

But signs of change were afoot: even then, the skyline was dominated by cranes for the many building projects underway. The real estate market had only opened to non-Gulf Cooperation Council nationals in 1999, so the Emirates were set for a period of rapid expansion.

Despite the culture shock, I found myself drawn in by Dubai. I was captured by the charm of the Old Town, Deira. I would watch the wooden *dhow* cargo boats dock right in front of the hotel, unloading crates of fruit, sacks of spices, and even motorbikes, which would have come from India or Iran, and observe people taking the water taxi across the Creek.

Soon after my arrival, I made friends and cultivated a vibrant social life. The city was full of young people. Some of our friends from Lebanon had moved to Dubai, as well, so we had a built-in network of people around us. We would go on outings outside the city when the weather was cooler. It was a good lifestyle for a young couple starting a family.

And in 1999, we welcomed our first child, Yasmine. When Zeina went into labor, I was at work. They called me and told me to come immediately. I was in such a rush that I drove my blue BMW right over the median next to the hospital, busting up the radiator. But at least I made it in time!

Around that time, a new director of sales and marketing joined, a South African guy named Sean Landing. He was introduced by our general manager, Henri, as a kind of messiah. And this was noteworthy because Henri hated everybody. In Lebanon we say, "He never smiled for a loaf of bread." Henri's morning meetings were just a laundry list of complaints blaming various departments for what went wrong the day before.

I joked, "I hope Sean Landing doesn't take off." Little did I know how right I would be. Six months later, he fled the country. And I do mean *fled*. He abandoned his apartment, left his car in the parking lot, and took a flight straight home.

It was unexpected, but not surprising: he didn't know Dubai, the market, or the accounts. Unable to handle the pressure Henri put on him, and perhaps overwhelmed by the fierce competition of the local hotel sector, Sean bailed before he could make an impact.

I thought, *This is my shot.* It was my chance to move into sales and marketing. It was a big leap. I hadn't worked in that capacity yet. But I was hungry, I had fresh ideas and drive, and I wanted the hotel to thrive—to reclaim its position atop the hotel rankings.

One morning, I approached Henri. "I want Landing's job," I said.

He shot me down. But I refused to take no for an answer. "I can do it—I know the city, I know the accounts, and I have the relationships. Give me a set of targets, and I'll make it happen."

Henri reluctantly agreed, accepting me on a probationary basis provided I could meet those targets. If not, I would be sacked. But there was also the matter of salary to resolve.

At the time I was making $2,000 per month. Landing was getting $5,000.

"I'll only do it if you give me Landing's salary," I said. "I'm the man for the job. Don't you think I'm worth the same money?" Fair is fair. I was, after all, taking on the same level of responsibility as my predecessor.

Henri balked, but I persisted. I was ready to walk if he refused again.

In the end, he relented, sort of. "I'll give you $4,000 a month and three months to hit the targets, and in three months, I'll bump you up to the $5,000 a month salary."

"There is no way I can do all that in three months," I countered. "Give me six months, and I'll do it."

We shook on it, and thus began my mission—and the ticking clock. It was a make-or-break career moment.

Initially, it was difficult. Not only did I have a daunting to-do list, but some of my peers were standing in my way.

First, some of the veterans in the department didn't immediately embrace me. They still saw me as a mid-level manager, and director of sales and marketing was an elite position. I would have to win them over, not only by excelling at my job, but by being personable; the kind of guy people enjoy working with. In hospitality, personality is key. You can't thrive on skills and experience alone. It's a people-based business, after all. That is as true for the back office as client-facing roles.

One colleague, in particular, seemed to have it in for me; the finance director, a man named Asif. He and I continually butted heads. He was much older than me, and I can only assume he resented the fact that I had been promoted to a high-level role at a young age. He was always after me, wanting to prove me wrong, challenge my numbers, or question my performance. Whatever I did, whatever I achieved, he always sought to undermine me.

Once, while I was on vacation with my family, he went behind my back to convince the general manager that the hotel was not performing well. I got wind of his scheme and had to leave my family vacation and come back to plead my case and correct the narrative.

As for the mission objectives, there were several problem areas that Henri entrusted me with solving. First, we had empty lobby showcases that no one was renting. Not only did this represent lost revenue, it created the wrong atmosphere. Empty showcases don't look good. They do not convey the feeling of prosperity and prestige that are part of the brand.

I approached luxury retailers like Rolex, Porsche, and Hugo Boss with a plan for renting space in our hotel. I found clients for all twenty spaces that had been sitting dormant, which brought in extra revenue and enriched the "first impression" for guests arriving at the hotel. It was especially rewarding to see Henri crack a rare smile when the final showcase was filled.

Second, we had lost two major corporate accounts, Kumho Tires and Nestlé. They used to be based close to the hotel but had moved to another part of the city when development on newer hotels started up, and the accounts moved with them. Henri wanted me to win back at least one.

Kumho Tires was a great account because they always had people flying in, staying at the hotel and entertaining clients for meetings and conferences. I managed to bring back Kumho within six months. Nestlé took more time to win over. Eventually, we sold them on the idea that the hotel points would be a valuable incentive to their employees. It was a generous package that benefited them tremendously but was still profitable for us. Within eight months, they were doing business with us again.

Those changes came down to our commitment to deliver unparalleled service and quality for their customers. We first focused on convincing them to use our space for their events, which paved the way to winning back their stayover guests who needed rooms.

In the mission to lure back Nestlé and Kumho, I relied on relationship building and cultivating a partnership with us through loyalty points, packages, and gift options. For instance, at the end of the year, corporate clients could use hotel points to shop for holiday gifts at any of the luxury showcases that now populated the lobby.

Third, I needed to clean up the sales team. One of the conditions I gave Henri was full authority to make staffing changes. There were several salespeople who had been sitting idle in their positions for years. They weren't goal-oriented. They were "farmers," planting and tending the fields, when we needed "hunters." After all, in sales, you eat what you kill, as they say.

The same way Henri gave me tasks, I delegated tasks to the sales team. I sat down with each salesperson and took a good hard look at their accounts. Together, we hit the pavement and visited those clients on-site, made introductions, and shored up longstanding relationships. We took clients to dinner and got to know their families. You have to get to know people on a personal level, not just business.

Through this process, I started to develop my own insights into how accounts were being managed—or mismanaged as it was in some cases.

One problem was that if an account was lost, sales team members rarely made the effort to assess why, much less to recover it. Moreover, people were often late for work or faked being sick. Some of them had simply become lazy or complacent after years in the position, and they couldn't keep up with the pace that a five-star hotel in a competitive market demands.

So, I set targets for the sales team. If you want to motivate people, you need to set specific goals, with the understanding that consequences will ensue if those targets aren't met. I gave several warnings to offenders to shape up or ship out. In the end, I had to fire three of the seven salespeople and replace them with young, ambitious employees with fire in their bellies.

My intention was not to go in guns blazing and kick people out of their jobs. Above all, I wanted to help people improve their performance and get everyone aligned with the same vision for growth. But for those three employees, termination was the only option.

The silver lining to an otherwise painful process of hiring and firing was that the remaining four salespeople also improved once they saw that underperformance would no longer be tolerated.

These staffing changes started to bear fruit as we won deal after deal and our clientele expanded. I made sure that we celebrated all our wins, big or small, as a *team*. I was hands on and joined them in celebrations and client meetings alike.

However, in the process, I provoked the wrath of Henri's wife. Some of the people who were let go during this period happened to be from the Philippines, which was also her country of birth. She took the firings personally and seemed to think I was "targeting" her compatriots. Of course, my decisions were purely performance-based, and the terminated employees had been given a chance to improve, but she would not hear it. She was sure I had it in for them. And any time she complained to Henri, I was sure to get an earful from him the next day.

It actually got so bad that Henri secretly decided he was not going to keep me on. But he didn't tell me about his plans; I was inadvertently tipped off by a friend!

"Are you leaving?" my friend asked one afternoon.

"No. Why?" I said.

"Oops, you didn't hear it from me then," he said. "But your position is posted on an online job board."

Irate, I went to Henri and asked for an explanation. He gave me an evasive, wishy-washy answer along the lines of, "We're just exploring other options."

I was upset. I had been achieving tremendous progress. I had to stand up for myself.

"You haven't told me I've underperformed. I have been meeting my targets," I said. He knew as well as I did that this was true.

In such moments, having allies, especially at the higher rungs, is priceless. Such relationships help ensure your professional longevity. I reached out to the corporate office, a guy called Dennis who was the regional VP of sales and who, by then, had started to take notice of the headway I was making. The conversation with Dennis reassured me that my position was safe. I also understood from that conversation that Henri was likely on the chopping block himself, but I kept that to myself.

The next thing Henri asked me to do was to introduce a program to get more guests to buy the club lounge offer. The hotel had a beautiful lounge, but people were mostly paying for the lower tier option and getting free upgrades. Club lounges across the industry will always be a cost to the hotel because it is essentially free food and drink, subsidized by the room rate. The goal was to offset those costs and make it as profitable as possible within the framework.

I developed a plan to monetize the lounge: club lounge members could still make use of the lounge and its benefits, but the new model required them to pay a supplement. In return, we gave guests better food, high tea, and other upscale benefits.

And lastly, there was the matter of rankings. That was the biggest task of all. The rankings are decided by Smith Travel Research (STR), which collects and audits hotel performance data and sets global benchmarks for the industry. They group and rank hotels by competitive set, with a minimum of five comparable hotels within the set. Inter-Continental Hotel was ranked fourth in Dubai, and Henri wanted us to become number one. It was time to reclaim the throne.

The performance of the hotel started to improve, but it really takes a year to turn something that sizeable and complex around— thankfully, Henri realized that. It meant shedding lower-rate contracts, winning new accounts, and putting together a new events team. It was a total strategic overhaul. We had to reimagine so much of what we did.

Ultimately, it took two years to make it to number one. Achieving that milestone was a big deal. Even more so because, at the same time, a lot of new hotels had opened up, the likes of the Grand Hyatt, Fairmont and the Emirates Towers, increasing the competition. But by reclaiming the top spot within the competitive set, we reaffirmed our status as a legacy, flagship hotel. Capitalizing on our history, elegance, and charm, we were outshining both the "old guard" and some of the new players in town.

The sense of accomplishment was strong. I felt that my team and I achieved everything we set to achieve. And more. But the bigger reward was the satisfaction of rising to the challenge. I had come in as an underdog. An underdog some people expected (even wanted) to fail. Instead, I had shown everyone that I was an asset to the team, the hotel, and the company as a whole.

I don't say any of this to brag, but simply to offer an example for other folks, especially younger workers, who are also looking for that elusive career break, whether in hospitality or some other field.

Given the renewed success of the hotel, we started getting more visits from the corporate office. People would ask me, "How did you do it? What was the strategy? Who are the team members?" They were studying what we had done to replicate it elsewhere. They were impressed I had come from operations and parachuted successfully into sales, in a role that my predecessor had fled.

By this time, Henri had been ushered into retirement. Sadly, he didn't get to see our great achievement of reclaiming our number one position in the market within our competitive set, and we had a new general manager, Tom Meyer. Tom was a friendly and charming German-Australian, and we got on well, right from the start. He was tall, stocky, and good looking, a marketeer through and through. He was selfless and extremely well spoken. If you put him on stage without a script, he could riff off the cuff and blow everyone's mind.

When asked about how sales had been able to turn things around, he liked to say, "I unleashed Haitham." After Henri departed, it was Tom who reiterated to me, "We want to stay number one. Whatever you need, you can have. Just get it done."

Things were going really well. On the personal front, our family had welcomed one more, as my son Karim was born three years after his sister. Yasmine was so excited about having a brother. She was very motherly toward him and treated him like a precious stuffed toy.

On the professional front, despite our success, I was still getting pushback from Asif, the finance director. He tried to get Tom on his side but it was Tom who put Asif in his place. When he would file complaints against me, Tom would simply ask him for facts to back up his claims, and I would plead my case by citing objective data. Tom would study both sets of facts (Asif's and mine) and judge accordingly. The numbers spoke for themselves. The hotel was performing better than ever. After that, Asif finally left me alone.

I learned a lot about marketing from Tom, who, despite having a lot on his plate in a new role in a new city, made time to educate me. He was an effective leader. He saw the good in people and gave them the benefit of the doubt. As my mother used to say, "If someone doesn't have an excuse, give them one." Tom felt that way, too. It was how he positioned things and made you look at problems differently; the glass was always half full.

And my own glass, already more than half full, was about to overflow. A dinner in 2004 made sure of that.

InterContinental Hotel Dubai had just opened a restaurant called Mystizo. It was a Latin-Mediterranean fusion place, which was a novel concept in Dubai at the time. At the opening, Tom put me next to Chris Moloney, our CEO. I felt immensely privileged just to be seated next to him.

For a high-profile executive, Chris was an understated guy. Short in stature, blonde, the picture of "smart casual" style, dressed in chinos and a blue blazer. He broke the ice with a funny story about his dog.

As the first course was being served, he turned to me and said, "You know, I've heard a lot about you and that you've done a great job here." He commended me for bringing the hotel back to number one. I felt proud. And we hit it off. As we ate and drank our way through the tasting menu, we talked about family, school, and compared notes about our lives in the U.S. I was captivated. In disbelief at how far I had come. I was having dinner with the CEO!

Not long after, he summoned me for a face-to-face meeting. I had never been to the corporate office before. I was a mix of nerves and excitement when I entered his office and sat down.

"We're proud of what you're doing, and we want you to join us here," he told me. I almost fell off my seat.

"Are you serious?" I asked.

He was. He offered me the director of sales and marketing role for the Mideast and Africa. Then I really did fall off my seat. That would put me in charge of 90 hotels across the two regions. And all my "competitors" at the other flagship hotels would be reporting to me.

To say I was flattered, would be an understatement.

They brought me my contract. I flipped to the last page and signed.

"Wait, wait, don't you want to read it? Don't you want to know what we'll pay you?" Chris asked.

"I'm sure it's generous. I just want the job."

Chris laughed. "You really should read it first."

"I'm good. When do I start?"

That promotion was a quantum leap in my career, and it all happened because I had persuaded a higher-up to take a chance on me, and persuaded *myself* that I was worth the gamble.

I learned a lot from that experience. First and foremost, it's hard to get to the top, but even harder to stay there. You cannot get comfortable, or the competition will knock you off your perch. You have to keep performing and advancing towards your goals.

I also learned not to count your chickens before they hatch. There was a time when we thought we had made it to the number one ranking, and we celebrated prematurely. When the report came out, we were actually listed as number two. And that left us with egg on our face.

And, lastly, regardless of how good you are, you cannot do anything without a great team. Play to your strengths, and let others fill in the gaps. In high school, I played football as a wide receiver. I could not play defense or quarterback or anything else, but I could run fast. It's the same in business. You compete as a team, and you win together. Before moving onto the next thing, you must give credit where credit is due. Recognize people for their achievements.

These lessons helped me win on two fronts: boost the status of the hotel and earn a place for me in the corporate office. Such is the world of hospitality. There is immense opportunity if you are willing to be bold, show true grit, and take positive action. Be a good person, do what needs doing, and recognition will follow. It is simply a matter of seizing your moment and taking a leap of faith.

CHAPTER 5

BIG MARKET, SMALL WORLD

A bu al-Hasan al-Masudi lived over a thousand years ago, but by dedicating his life to the study of the history, geography, ecology, and anthropology of the Muslim world, he left behind a wealth of knowledge, which scholars still consult today. Al-Masudi was a rarity: a Renaissance man before the Renaissance, who traveled far and wide, by land and sea, from bustling, golden-age Baghdad—the city of his birth—to Syria, Armenia, Oman, Sri Lanka, India, Iran, and even to the distant shores of Zanzibar.

Besides his exhaustive travels and insatiable thirst for knowledge, what made al-Masudi such a prolific scholar was his gift for *listening*. He spoke not only with learned men, but traders, artisans, travelers, and ordinary people he met on the way, exchanging information and using what they told him of their own culture and locale to broaden his understanding. And, as he wrote in one book, "to learn the peculiarities of various nations and parts of the world."

Now, a millennium later, I found myself following in al-Masudi's footsteps, traversing the same countries, and gathering knowledge through travel, dialogue, and research. Okay, my trade was sales and marketing rather than history and geography, and instead of ancient royal courts and university libraries lit by candlelight, I was consorting with hotel general managers and corporate executives. But in my own small way, I had joined the ancient tradition of those itinerant Muslim and Arab scholars who wanted to understand the world by venturing far beyond their own front doors.

It was still an office job, but depending on the week, that office could be Amman, Addis Ababa, Anatolia, or Accra. In my previous role, I went on business trips two or three times a year. Now I was on the road two to three times per month.

Of course, the promotion came with a lot of perks *and* a big uptick in responsibilities. I was now overseeing 90 hotels instead of one. The hours were long, the stress was great, and not all my colleagues were, initially, welcoming. Since I was now working with 90 hotel sales directors across the region, that meant 90 experts who thought their way was the right way, 90 egos, 90 personalities, 90 different agendas. And not all of them wanted me to succeed. Thankfully, a few did.

Overnight, I found myself in the awkward position of managing people who used to be my peers, some of them many years older than me. That was a challenge for both of us. I had to strike a delicate balance between exerting the authority necessary to do my job while being deferential and respectful of their own seniority. To be confident and to lead without being arrogant or domineering. And, in the first months, there was no room for error: I had to prove to everyone that I deserved the promotion, which meant working longer and harder and putting all my heart into it.

No one really confronted me directly, but there were a lot of doubters on the sidelines who were not happy I got the position. The reality is that, any time a coveted role opens up in a corporate structure, only one person gets picked, and others who felt they were next in line are going to feel jilted. Most folks move on, but some hold a grudge.

So, there was a lot of "Why did he get the job?" skepticism. Which made my life difficult because I was always starting on the back foot.

My father, who had gathered a lot of wisdom about handling people during decades in the cutthroat business world, gave me sage advice. "I'm extremely proud of you Haitham, but tread lightly because these are the times when people, especially those closest to you, become envious. And envy is your biggest enemy."

He also urged me to look inward as well as outward. "Be careful of your own ego. You deserve this opportunity. You're qualified, without question. But don't think you're better than everyone. You were there at the right time and right place. Others might have just as easily been chosen. You're not *lucky*. You earned this role on the basis of your own skill and hard work. But you *are* fortunate. Never forget that."

I took his words to heart.

THE JOURNEYS OF A HOTELIER

Business travel can be a grind, sure, especially when it means leaving your family at home. But it was also a rush, so enriching to be exposed to different cultures and observe how each country or region's way of life impacted their approach to hospitality. My professional education ramped up rapidly.

Life became a succession of packing and unpacking as I dashed between trade shows, exhibitions, meetings with other hotel managers, sit-downs with tour operators and bookers, and countless coffees, teas, lunches, and dinners with hotel stakeholders of all types. You had to be a quick study and absorb a lot of information about individual hotel practices as well as cultural nuances of the particular location.

Amman, Jordan was one destination I visited several times. It was still kind of underdeveloped in terms of retail infrastructure or F&B. There weren't that many restaurants of note, and little in the way of shopping beyond a mall or two. People bought what they needed in traditional souks selling domestic products. Strolling through the maze-like marketplace, you'd get lost among the plethora of traditional sweet shops, herb stores, and old-school bakeries: a carousel of smells, flavors, textures, and colors.

Amman has changed a lot since then. The city hasn't lost its traditions or its old-world charm—you can still spend hours finding bargains in the souks—but the city is more developed and cosmopolitan, with more to appeal to the average middle-class consumer,

What struck me about Amman was its historical richness. The company booked us on a lot of tours so we could get familiar with the country. I visited a nearly 2,000-year-old church, where I felt awe-struck imagining how many worshippers prayed there over the centuries. And I walked in the very spot on the banks of the Jordan River where Jesus himself was baptized.

The Dead Sea was a marvel. There is no place like it on earth. It gets its name from the high salinity of the water, so salty that virtually nothing can live in it. This also makes the water unusually buoyant so that you float more easily. The texture of the water was oily, almost like kerosene. If it gets in your eyes, it burns like hell. And Dead Sea mud is known for its healthful properties. It was amusing to see my colleagues, normally so buttoned-up and professional, in bathing suits, slathering each other with mud.

The Dead Sea is the lowest point on earth, which means the concentration of oxygen is greater, so you feel more refreshed. In the evenings, the sun sets, the breeze rolls through, and you just feel physically good all through your body. It's invigorating.

Jordanian cuisine is incredible, boasting such delectable dishes as *mansaf* (a rice and lamb platter) and *makloubeh* (a medley of gently spiced vegetables and chicken or lamb served with yogurt salad). Impeccable Jordanian hospitality matches the quality of the food. I mean "hospitality" not in the sense of "hotels" but in the original sense of the word: the culture of welcoming strangers with warmth and generosity, opening your doors to them and offering a seat at your table, sharing food, culture, and laughter.

Other times I journeyed to Africa, a continent I had never visited before. Addis Ababa, the densely populated capital of Ethiopia, was a highlight. Addis is as high as the Dead Sea is low: 2,300m (7,500 feet) above sea level, so the air is thinner. It takes time to get acclimated. When working out in the hotel gym I had to be careful that I didn't get so winded I'd fall off the treadmill!

Ethiopia, like Jordan, has a rich religious and cultural heritage. It is a proud civilization that dates back millennia and houses many sites important to early Christianity. Ethiopian cuisine is a medley of powerful flavors that you won't forget once you've tried it. The typical meal consists of several small dishes of lentils, vegetables, chicken, or beef flavored with turmeric, fenugreek, cumin, garlic, besobela, and rosemary, served atop spongey *injera* bread. It's hard to describe: a cross between the flavors of the Middle East, India, and East Africa, which makes sense considering its geography.

While in Jordan I ate till bursting point, it was difficult to do the same in Addis. Although I love connecting with different cultures through food, surprisingly, Addis didn't have many restaurants offering local authentic food. Instead, I had most of my meals in an Italian place near the hotel. To call it authentic Italian was a stretch but no matter where you are in the world, it's hard to mess up pasta.

I also took opportunities to travel with my family for pleasure, and my kids grew accustomed to the lifestyle of planes and hotels. During one trip to London, where we stayed at the InterContinental Hotel Park Lane. Five-year-old Yasmine ran into the suite, jumped on the bed, and exclaimed, "I love my life!"

Me too, Yasmine, I thought, grateful for the opportunity to share all this with my family.

THE MISSION

I wish I could say I got paid just to tour ancient churches and indulge in the local cuisine, but these trips were hard work, vital to keeping the sales and marketing engine humming. Hospitality is a competitive business. Every day you contend with threats both internally and externally. You can't let your guard down.

When I started, I had several big challenges to tackle.

Consistency was a big one. In a large international hotel chain like IHG, there is a tension between the global/corporate and the local. You have branding specifications, pricing structures, and global SOPs to adhere to, but you also have to account for cultural differences and the need to allow hotel sales teams the flexibility to do what they do best. After all, they understand their own market better than anyone.

My predecessors didn't spend enough time in field; they preferred to stay closer to home, in our corporate office in Dubai. So, one of the changes I implemented was getting on the ground/in the field more to identify solutions and find alignment between the individual locations and the organization as a whole.

It was tempting for some hotels to "go rogue" in their approach and try to gobble up the biggest share of accounts by diverting from company SOPs. But there is a reason those SOPs exist—if everyone flouts the rules, then the organization suffers. It's like playing soccer: if one player cheats for his own benefit, he may gain. But if everyone does the same, you no longer have a game, you have an anarchic free-for-all.

So, individual hotels skirting the rules added to the pressure on us because when we would audit sales and marketing, we found inconsistencies, and this made it hard to measure and improve performance.

Every hotel would insist, "Yeah but we're different. We can't follow the same playbook as everyone else." That was half-true. Those policies were created at the corporate level to be flexible enough to accommodate the interests and challenges of individual hotels as well as disparate cultural contexts.

How did I resolve this dissonance?

In the hotel business, you can broadly break down sales into two categories: national and global. Global accounts had an umbrella agreement with IHG that applied across the region they would travel to. For example, if a big company like Cisco is renting rooms in the UAE, Egypt, and Lebanon, they want an agreement that applies for the whole region, so they know what to expect in terms of cost and service and don't have to negotiate with individual establishments.

National sales pertain to local accounts. That's the area where you can allow more slack for hotels to do what they want. For example, a local account that doesn't have requirements for international travel but needs rooms for visiting regional clients requires the hotel team to cultivate interpersonal relationships. There's a lot of competition over prime accounts, and ultimately, people don't choose where to stay based on price and star rating alone. They go with who they feel good about and trust.

Another of my missions was to overhaul our sales and marketing strategy. Chris hired me because I was passionate about my work and had a reputation as a problem solver and creative thinker. So, I was expected to do a lot more than just steer the ship; I had to find new routes of passage. To be an explorer in strange lands, like al-Masudi.

Some people think that if you're promoted to a high-level role like director or executive, you're the big bad boss man and you should just charge in giving orders, making changes, and telling people what's what. This is untrue in hospitality and generally the wrong approach in any industry.

Listen *first*, then act.

That was the biggest part of my job in those first years: listening. Not only is this the best way to gather information—God gave you two ears and one mouth—but it also demonstrates respect for others, which helps earn their admiration and trust.

Above all, don't be a "preacher"—someone who thinks he knows everything about everything.

As I traveled from country to country, hotel to hotel, I observed, listened, asked questions, and learned the general managers' and sales managers' trade. I took notes on what was working and what wasn't. Each new place I visited, I picked up new techniques.

From that, I was able to develop a set of best practices that could be adapted to and shared with the rest of the organization. I had a hand in all the hotels in the Middle East and Africa, which included several different brands under the IHG umbrella. So, my broad, general knowledge was synthesized with their deep, localized knowledge to furnish something new which could then be shared throughout the organization.

After a while, we had a fully stocked toolkit which could be used all over. Which meant I could fly into one market, encounter a similar situation I had seen elsewhere, and simply ask the hotel managers "Have you tried this?" There's no better way to earn trust and buy-in than helping people solve problems.

Being a director isn't only about problem solving; it's also about recognizing when people are doing things right and leaving well enough alone. If a hotel was thriving, the best approach was to leave them alone. If it ain't broke, don't fix it. That also helped me earn the support of the hotel managers, because nothing raises people's ire more than someone from corporate micromanaging or creating solutions to problems that don't exist.

I mentioned before how people in the business *thrive* on recognition, so when a higher-up doles out praise for a job well done, they are elated.

One rule I followed was to avoid making things complex for the sake of complexity. That's a common pitfall among directors in any field. More complex doesn't mean better and, in fact, is often worse. Simplification is elegant and efficient. Less is more.

This rule is also important when implementing changes that affect people's workday. That's another challenge for corporate higher ups: change management. People are creatures of habit and resist when you ask them to alter a practice they've done for years. But they are more willing to adapt to simpler solutions than complex ones.

In 2006, I was part of the team who worked on uplifting the Holiday Inn brand. Many of these changes were cosmetic, such as altering the font of the logo and what we called soft-light uplift to the brand standards.

Holiday Inn was introduced to the region in 1971, and whoever was responsible for translating the brand name into Arabic omitted the "A," so that it read "Holidy Inn", which reads as هوليدي إن. I took advantage of our overhaul to correct this error by adding an Arabic A, so that it would be هوليداي إن.

Some of the veterans complained. "We have had it spelled that way since the seventies, why are you changing it?" There was no reason to keep it; it looked bad. Imagine walking into the lobby of your hotel and looking up to see "Holidy Inn" above the reception counter. You'd probably walk right back out and pick a hotel that can spell its own name correctly! In a business where attention to detail is paramount, we can't ignore the small things. When you start overlooking the small things, you end up overlooking the big things too.

And even if you're not an Arabic speaker, I hope the next time you stay in a Holiday Inn in the Middle East, you appreciate the change!

CASE STUDY: OUR WINTER, YOUR SUMMER

I made several business trips to Lebanon during those years. It was poignant to return to the city and country of my birth, which, although having recovered from the civil war, still bore some signs of that conflict, such as building facades pockmarked by bullet holes. Despite the scars of the past, Lebanon was doing well in those years, which were peaceful and prosperous.

In IHG's InterContinental Phoenicia, the flagship hotel in the region, the marketing team was struggling with a common problem: how to boost business during the laggard off-season. During summer, occupancy was high, but in the winter months, many rooms sat empty.

They developed a marketing campaign targeting Middle Eastern tourists, who make up a quarter of the country's inbound visitors.[3] These were people from warmer climates who during winter flocked to the grand cities and

---

3   Edmund Bower, "Lebanon reports visitor increase despite border conflict," *Arabian Gulf Business Insight*, March 20, 2024, *https://www.agbi.com/tourism/2024/03/lebanon-reports-visitor-increase-despite-border-conflict/*

world-class ski resorts of Europe, especially high spending travelers from the Gulf region.

They had the clever idea of marketing Lebanon as a winter destination. The Mediterranean country is famous for its beaches and warm weather, but it also has snow-capped mountains, ski resorts, and cozy chalets. Most tourists from abroad had no *idea* Lebanon offered all this. But once we got the word out, our hotels in Beirut and other destinations in Lebanon got busy again during the off-season.

Later, I adapted that same approach to the UAE market, and tweaked it to appeal to the European market: instead of shivering on some snowy mountaintop, spend the winter in the UAE, which is mild and pleasant. "Our winter, your summer" was the tagline.

We combined these ideas into a "marketing toolkit" of turnkey solutions, applicable to all markets. It provided the essential materials while giving hotels free reign with the imagery so that they could tailor the presentation to their locale.

My time in Beirut was extended when the company posted me there for a year and a half in 2009-2010 as both area general manager for Lebanon and commercial director Near East (an area that included Lebanon, Jordan, and Egypt). The role united both commercial and operations, which is unusual in the industry.

At the same time as my appointment, a new GM was hired at the Phoenicia. He was an Austrian, Georg, who loved his whiskey and smoked like a chimney—a habit that sadly, eventually cost him his life due to lung cancer. Georg ran things like a dictator and adamantly did not want me involved in his hotel. He convinced his hotel owners that he was best left to run it on his own and not fall under any area leadership. Instead of reporting to me, as he was supposed to, he would report directly to IHG'S corporate, a man called Pascal, who was VP Operations at the time. But Lebanon was not under his remit. Georg's main goal was to keep me out of the Phoenicia at all costs.

These conflicts were tough, but I managed. They were also good training for how to deal with people. A lesson I would have to apply soon when I faced one of the biggest crises of my career.

CHAPTER 6

THE CHAMELEON

I'll never win an Oscar, but I can imagine what it must feel like. Donning your tux and, accompanied by your elegantly dressed wife or partner, gathering in a ballroom with hundreds of your industry peers. Marveling at all the pomp and circumstance. The suspense as you wait for the announcement of the winners, and the satisfaction of hearing the emcee call you up to the stage to a rousing round of applause.

This was the scene that capped off my first year in the job in 2006, when I was honored with the Best Local Marketing Activity Award for the whole EMEA region (Europe, Middle East, and Africa) at a black-tie gala in Stockholm. The idea that made the award possible was a campaign targeting business travelers with a new service at hotels called the Crowne Plaza Personalized Concierge. With this promotion, we encouraged business travelers to book executive rooms, which then gave them access to a dedicated concierge service pre, during and after their stay. They had only to call a single number to handle everything from airport pickup, business meetings, printing documents, blocking meeting space, and making restaurant reservations. While unique in the market at the time, it is now a basic requirement of every business traveler.

It put me on the map and helped extinguish the remaining doubt among colleagues who questioned my capability. When people see you up on stage being recognized by company bigwigs for your achievement, it means something.

Chris Moloney, a man I looked up to, and the one who enabled my rapid jump to the corporate position, moved on when I was a year into the job. His replacement was a gentleman we will call, for discretion's sake, John, an ex-rugby player from the UK who hardly ever smiled.

John and I got on really well, initially, but after a while I observed he had a tendency to be over-critical, not just of me but of everyone.

One day, I was in his office when he was lecturing me about something, and he said, in a way that was both facetious and condescending, "You have a lot to learn, Haitham."

"I am learning. Wait and see, John. One day I'm gonna have your job."

He chuckled and said, "Okay, get out of here."

The exchange was light-hearted, but there was a faint undercurrent of tension that seemed to presage rockier relations.

And sure enough, things did go south. His critiques become more strident. He had a habit of putting me down and made me feel I wasn't good enough for the role. We didn't see eye to eye, and we didn't like each other.

This was especially frustrating because I continued to thrive in the role. Each year I was either nominated or won an award, from a pool of more than 400 sales/marketing people across the EMEA region. It didn't matter.

John was unimpressed by all this. He called me a "poser" and said I had a big ego, a criticism which no one had ever raised before.

It was ironic because John had an ego as big as the Burj Khalifa.

Even though I *knew* his harsh words were untrue, they got under my skin. And once I internalized them, I started to doubt myself. Maybe I *wasn't* good enough. Or maybe my good fortune had finally run out and, after a decade of rapid career growth, I had gotten as far as I ever would. That's the fate of many people in corporate—they get a few promotions but then stall out, get stuck in the same position and slog slowly toward retirement.

This kind of pessimistic thinking was contrary to my nature, but I was really struggling with self-doubt.

By 2011, our relationship hit a low point. I started seeking transfers to other regions, especially Europe. But John obstructed that too, because he refused to recommend me for any role. Damned if you do, damned if you don't. I felt trapped.

He was impacting not just my career, but my emotional wellbeing.

This is not an uncommon workplace scenario: dealing with a toxic boss. It really can ruin your life, because we do spend about half our waking hours in the office, and a toxic work situation can occupy your thoughts, even when you're *not* at work.

Generation Z employees have been portrayed in the press as less willing to put up with toxicity, but that paints things with a broad brush. If you're a young person who hasn't been in the workforce long, and don't have much clout in your office, you might be more vulnerable to a bullying or undermining manager. Dealing with this requires particular skills which they don't teach in school, and which usually come only with experience.

What can one do in these circumstances? Often, people end up suffering in silence, but this only prolongs the problem. Confronting the guilty party is an option, but confrontation also requires finesse to avoid making a bad problem worse. Plus, if the offending party refuses to change, what is your next move? Short of quitting, not much.

I was at a loss, so I sought help through IHG's human resources department. Jenny was VP of HR, a well-rounded professional and great adviser to John. She really knew and understood people and how to help guide them through challenges.

I told her the situation. "John and I got along at the beginning and he supported my career journey but then things soured. I don't remember where it went wrong but something broke. I don't know how to fix it."

She told me to have a heart-to-heart with John. Communication solves most problems. Even bullies are sometimes willing to listen and try to correct course. Rare is the manager who *wants* to stir up conflict in the office. And I don't think that's what John was doing—he wasn't *trying* to make life hard on me. But he definitely needed some behavior modification.

So, the next day I knocked on his door and said, "John, I've got a stone in my shoe. I need to sit down and talk about it."

He beckoned me in, and I gave it to him straight. "Things were good between us at first, but it's changed. We're not in a good place."

He didn't reciprocate my candor, preferring instead to equivocate and dance around the topic. John didn't like any kind of direct confrontation and communication was not his strong suit. The conversation ended without me getting through to him.

I reported back to Jenny that my attempt at dialogue had failed, so she set me up with a life coach, paid for by the company. This was a man who was highly regarded (his hefty fee reflected that). I was grateful that IHG cared enough about my well-being to cover the expense. Of course, it's in their interest, too, because interpersonal strife and low morale, especially among high-level personnel, is bad for business.

I felt a little awkward when I showed up for my first appointment with the coach, having never been in this situation before. It felt more like meeting a shrink. He had a practice in his small sitting room in his villa. Mostly I talked as he listened and pushed me to reflect.

Then he gave his assessment: "I think the root of the problem is that you intimidate John."

"What do you mean?" I asked.

"Well, think. You tell me. What might I mean by that?" That's what a good therapist or coach is trained to do. Not spoon-feed you answers, but guide you to scrutinize your own problem and infer your own conclusions.

Was John intimidated by me? That would explain his puzzling accusations that I had an inflated ego. Perhaps he was projecting his own evaluation of me. It kind of made sense.

For example, I was a sharp dresser; John was more casual, bordering on careless. I wore a suit every day. I never thought of this as an indulgence—when you're meeting clients and representing the company all day, you should dress the part—but did that come across to John as somehow flashy?

The coach said, "Stop doing things that intimidate him. What if you dress down a little bit? Keep the suit but lose the handkerchief and tie. Maybe wear some chinos like John."

"But I don't like chinos."

"Just try it. Mirror him," he advised.

So, I changed my style of dress. Not to emulate John as I needed to remain myself, but at least be less sartorially intimidating. I kept the suit with a white button-down shirt but left the tie at home, unless I had a client meeting.

Still, for John that was a little too formal. *Mirror him.* I heard the coach's voice in my head. I noticed John would walk around the office without his suit jacket. So, I did the same: my uniform became trousers, pressed white shirt, but no jacket. I still wasn't wearing chinos.

After a month or two, John went to Jenny and said, "Haitham has changed a lot. He's different. I like it, I think."

Jenny relayed the comment to me. "I don't know what you're doing, but it's working."

I said, "You'll never believe it. One simple trick..."

Jenny laughed. It *was* so remarkably simple, yet seemed to make all the difference.

It does make sense after all, right? Perception is reality. And no one understands that better than people in the hotel business. Appearance counts. Details matter. What you communicate outwardly, and aesthetically, dictates how you are seen internally. Hotels spend millions carefully curating the décor of their lobbies and reception areas to create a certain mood or vibe, set the tone (opulent, hip and casual, snappy and efficient, no-frills practical, etc.), and craft an aura of professionalism.

So, my relationship with John had *improved* but there was still a lot of friction.

I continued the sessions with the life coach, who recommended a book to me, *Taming Your Gremlin* by Richard Carson. The book teaches how to suppress the voice of negativity that sometimes sabotages you (the gremlin) and prevents you from reaching your potential. It stresses self-awareness, observing your own thoughts and feelings, and creative visualization as a means of embracing change, to become the person you want to be.

Reading it was eye-opening and I recognized in those pages many of the same habits I had unknowingly cultivated, especially the whip of self-doubt. The one we often use to beat ourselves up even when there's no justification for it. "Self-doubt" is a slippery term because often its origin is not in the self, but, as in my case, in others. The unwanted voice in my head was mostly John's. I had internalized his criticisms and made them my own.

Since then, I've recommended that book to many people who need to regain their confidence or silence their internal voice of self-destruction.

I put the lessons of the book into practice in my daily life. That gave me a kind of armor against negativity, against my gremlin, and, as a result, John's barbs had less of an impact on me.

I used to drive a Porsche 911, which also elicited disparaging or undermining comments from John. Comments that suggested I was putting on airs, showing off, or not "staying in my place" because I was a "mere" director, and he was the CEO. Never mind the fact that he drove a flashy

Aston Martin, a vehicle that was much more of a look-at-me status symbol than my car! It didn't matter.

I wasn't sentimentally attached to the car, so just as I had with my tailored suits and silk ties, I traded it in for a more modest vehicle.

At after work drinks one day a colleague said to me, "Hey man, I heard you sold your car."

"Oh yeah, I didn't use it so much, so I figured I'd downsize," I bluffed.

John overheard, and I could tell by his expression he was happy by the news.

This might all seem petty, even juvenile, but humans are funny creatures. As much as we like to think we are cool, rational, level-headed beings, we are influenced by emotion and whim as much as any other factor. And just because you're nearing the top of the corporate pyramid doesn't mean personality (and clashes between personalities) doesn't play a role. Personality becomes even *more* of a factor. Egos tend to get even bigger up in the C-suite.

You just have to learn how to read and handle people. I had been doing that all my career, ever since I would sit back and observe the psychological "ecosystem" of the kitchen and the washroom. How people interacted, what made them tick, what was needed, what they liked. My relationship with John was a new challenge, but I learned new techniques to navigate it successfully.

Between the inward work of self-awareness and positive self-talk, and the outward work of presenting myself a little more modestly, I had tamed the saboteur within me and the saboteur in the corner office down the hall.

Amidst all this, I did do some serious introspection about my career.

One day I got an email from a headhunter I had met before, working on behalf of Hilton Corporation. He was looking for a VP for sales and marketing for Middle East, Africa, Turkey, Russia and Eastern Europe. I read the job description and immediately called back with great excitement. I knew just the guy for the role.

"Hi, Haitham here, calling about your email. The person you're looking for: that's me."

"I was hoping you'd say that," he said.

The situation with John had abated enough that I didn't feel I needed to change workplaces to get away from him. But there were other reasons calling to me. After many years specializing in the regional market, I wanted to broaden my horizons. I didn't want to be pigeonholed as "the Mideast guy." And this position was exactly what I was looking for in my career.

MOVING FROM IHG TO HILTON

They booked me on a flight to London, where the interview would be conducted. Before I flew out, I spoke to Hilton's Michael Prager, a stocky Jewish Englishman, who was leading the search committee. He left a good impression on me from the first moment we spoke. I expressed that I really wanted this job. I asked "What is this panel looking for?"

He said, "Focus on what you would do in your first 90 days. How will you transform this sales community. If you can put something together that shows you have a vision, you'll be in a good position."

That's such an invaluable "interview hack" a lot of job seekers don't consider: you don't have to go into the interview blind. If you want to know the kinds of questions you can expect and the qualities they are searching for, just ask!

The flight from Dubai to London is eight hours, ample time to review my notes, reflect on how far I had come, and where I might be going next if I landed this job. The interview was taking place at the Hilton London Heathrow airport hotel. I was only in London for the day, but at reception, I asked for a room so I could rest up, refresh, and do some last-minute prep.

I told the receptionist I was there for an interview with Michael Prager.

"Oh, are you Mr. Amit?" she asked.

"Nope," I said—but now I knew who my competitor was!

As I mentioned, hospitality is a small village at global scale. Everyone is acquainted with everyone else, especially at the SVP/director/executive level. And I happened to know Amit. Great guy, I liked him. But I knew he wasn't a threat because he had a much smaller remit than me (overseeing a much more compact area.) And I was working for what was the world's largest hotel company in the world then, IHG. That put me at ease a little.

The interview was conducted by Michael, who was SVP of sales and marketing, the VP of revenue management, and the VP of marketing for Europe, Middle East & Africa.

For the next 90 minutes, I did a presentation to the panel of three executives on my vision for sales and marketing in the region, emphasizing the areas that Michael had highlighted were of particular interest to the higher-ups. That's also key—whether you're doing stand-up comedy, or vying for a coveted VP role with a new company, you must "play to your audience."

I poured out all the knowledge I had accumulated from doing sales and marketing for the past decade—how we can expand market share and increase revenue per available room (RevPar) and what personnel we need to acquire and develop. My IHG role had given me exposure to sales, marketing, PR, and revenue management, whereas at Hilton, these functions were mostly siloed—managers and execs specialized in one but had little involvement in the other. This was a crucial advantage because I was able to present myself as more well-rounded, someone who could thrive in my wheelhouse—sales and marketing—while also integrating the other areas into a comprehensive commercial strategy.

As I wrapped up the presentation, I held my breath and waited. Michael had a gleam in his eye that seemed to suggest, "Well done, Haitham." The other two were poker-faced. Then they launched into their deluge of questions. I was like a PhD candidate presenting my dissertation to an academic board—they put every aspect of my presentation under the microscope, throwing tough questions my way and hitting me with various devil's advocate-type scenarios to test the viability of my ideas. Gauging, I suppose, if I really knew my stuff, or if I had just had an assistant put the presentation together.

Moreover, they wanted to "stress test" my plan to ascertain if I had a vision for how to *execute it*. It's one thing to put a bunch of nice-sounding ideas up on a PowerPoint, but if you haven't thought through how to enact them, it doesn't do any good.

At IHG, I had really excelled as someone who was skilled in both strategy and execution. People recognized me as both a thinker and a doer. At the interview I had to be convincing that I could tackle both sides; otherwise, they would have seen my presentation as a lot of board room hot air.

When it concluded, we shook hands and I thanked them for the opportunity. I knew I had done well, but I had no idea how the other two candidates fared.

Michael and I had dinner that evening, before I flew home. He could hardly wait to tell me: "You got the job, mate. It's you."

Back in Dubai, I contemplated how I'd tell John I was leaving. That's never an easy conversation to have. I wasn't sure how he'd react. Maybe with bitterness. Maybe he'd jump for joy, click his heels, and uncork some champagne—"Finally I don't have to deal with Haitham and his suits!"

But to my surprise, when I broke the news, I could see, for the first time, he felt remorse. And when my last week came, he organized an amazing farewell for me, during which he sang my praises, recounted my achievements, and wished me well in my next endeavor in a way that was heartwarming to me. This from the guy who dutifully avoided complimenting me for everything lest it "pump my ego." Maybe beneath that tough, critical exterior, he was a good guy. Perhaps he had admired me all along.

"A CHRISTIAN, A MUSLIM, AND A JEW WALK INTO A HOTEL BAR..."

My first trip as a VP with Hilton was to Palestine, modern day Israel. My job isn't political, but politics and international relations certainly impact tourism. And Israel and Lebanon have been long-time rivals. That means visitors of one country to the other are sometimes subject to scrutiny, or denied entry outright. I was traveling on a U.S. passport but all passports state your place of birth and, with a name like Haitham Mattar, I might as well have been called "Ahmad Mohammed." I was expecting some low-level harassment on arrival.

"Let's do the trip together. At least I'm Jewish," said Michael, only half-kidding.

Sure enough, when I landed at the airport the Israeli authorities bombarded me with a lot of questions, but I had nothing to hide. One female officer said, "Do you know anyone in the West Bank?"

"The West Bank? Where's that?"

She laughed. I knew all about the West Bank, of course, but I thought if I sounded ignorant, she may just let me pass. And she did!

Finally, I got past customs where Michael was waiting for me at the arrivals gate. We chuckled about it.

We stayed in Tel Aviv and visited Jerusalem. Jerusalem is an important city for three major religions, Christianity, Judaism, and Islam. It's the site of the famous al-Aqsa Mosque, one of Islam's holiest sites. I told Michael, I've gotta see that mosque!

"Listen mate, there's us three Jews and you. There's no way we can take you. You'll have to see it at a distance through the Jewish quarters."

Hilton was building a Waldorf Astoria hotel in Jerusalem at the time, so we visited the site and met with the owners. I kept droning on about visiting the mosque.

Later, Michael and the two other Jewish colleagues went to the Western Wall in the Old City to pray while I waited in the courtyard. As I waited for my colleagues to return, a rabbi in a long black robe approached me and, without warning, placed his hand on my forehead and started reading from a text.

"What's your name?" he asked.

"Haitham," I said.

"Who?!"

"Uh, David," I answered quickly.

"Okay, David. Can you help me out with getting something for dinner?"

"You want money?" I pulled out a fistful of shekels from my pocket and handed him a twenty.

"No, give me the hundred," he said. I was thinking, what, he wants prime rib for dinner?

By then Michael and the other two saw me and came running over and intervened. I gave the hungry rabbi the twenty and we walked on.

We went on to an elevated area in the vicinity of the Armenian Quarter, where, finally, I was able to lay my eyes on the top of the golden dome of the mosque, an iconic symbol for Muslims worldwide. I wasn't able to go inside, but just catching a glimpse of that landmark was deeply moving. It only cost me twenty shekels but perhaps I gained some blessings from a religious man!

That was one of many adventures I experienced in my five years at Hilton, a time in my career of great satisfaction and professional growth. I was given a free hand from Michael to implement the strategy that I presented to the interview panel. And Michael was an excellent boss. He was gracious, patient, and invested in my success. We had a great mutual respect: he deferred to my expertise about the Middle East and Africa while mentoring me in the Turkish, Russian and European markets that were new to me. I also learned a lot about sales and marketing in general from him. He was a true expert with a lot of wisdom.

I had over a hundred hotels in my region and a couple hundred sales team members, including eight direct reports. Geographically, the region stretched from Moscow all the way down to the tip of South Africa in Cape Town, and everything in between, plus the Middle East, Israel, and Turkey.

It was an opportune time to serve as VP because Hilton was expanding its empire. Four years before I came in, Blackstone had acquired Hilton and the acquisition sparked growth. That year, Hilton added a bevy of hotels in Africa and Europe to its portfolio, which caused it to leapfrog IHG as the largest hotel company in the world.[4]

As a new captain on board the ship, I hoisted the "sales" to take advantage of these tailwinds and venture to new horizons.

First, I opened a sales office in Moscow and launched campaigns to appeal to Russians, who have a strong appetite for overseas travel, especially to places like the UAE, the Maldives, or the Seychelles.

I also researched overlooked markets with strong "outbound" numbers (tourists traveling abroad). I established a sales presence in the Czech Republic (now Czechia) and Poland. Czechia was a small but lucrative market with a growing middle class. Poland was also a right time/right place situation, with the tenth biggest economy in Europe and a population of 40 million, many of whom had disposable income.

We also grew our footprint in Turkey as we opened new hotels in the major cities as well as smaller towns, which

---

4   Today Hilton Worldwide is third on the list, after Marriott and Shanghai-based Jin Jiang.

was a logistical challenge because, unlike in Istanbul or Ankara, there were few English speakers who could work reception and staff the hotel restaurant. So, we had to be resourceful and build out the tourist infrastructure there. When I left Hilton after five years, we were operating 50 hotels in Turkey, up from 17 when I came in.

Candidly, however, the job was not always a picnic. I contended with the same resistance and skepticism I had periodically encountered at IHG. Michael Prager was a rare bright spot in a work environment that was, at first, unwelcoming, characterized by deep-seated office politics and strong influence from long-standing leaders and certain departments. As a new joiner, this situation was particularly challenging. I took the time to identify and connect with colleagues who shared similar values and could offer support. Building relationships with these individuals created a network of allies who provided guidance and assistance, while fostering an environment that allowed work to get done, without backbiting and infighting.

At Hilton, the rejection from the old timers played out in several ways. These veterans, who had been with the company for decades, were deeply entrenched in their ways of working and skeptical of new ideas. They viewed any change as a threat. This resistance manifested in dismissive attitudes during meetings, reluctance to collaborate, and outright opposition to new initiatives.

To overcome this rejection and build credibility, I employed several strategies. First, I took the time to listen to their concerns. This made them feel heard and respected. By meeting individually with key veterans, I could address their specific worries and build personal connections. And I focused on achieving small, quick wins that demonstrated the effectiveness of my ideas without causing major disruptions. These successes gradually built trust.

Communication and relationship-building will let you thrive in any professional setting, particularly those characterized by complex dynamics. You can't control what others do or think or say; you can only control what *you* do. Maintaining integrity and empathy and gradually turning rivals to supporters, and supporters to friends, will help you weather whatever workplace storm swirls around you. Yeah, it can be frustrating, especially when you're the new guy, but stick to these principles and tough it out.

Sadly, Michael decided to retire from Hilton 24 months after my joining and I then had a new boss to report to. One without Michael's excellence or charm. It was a challenging time for me to move from working with a sales and marketing pro to an absolute amateur.

Only after I left did the true impact of my initiatives and the value I brought to Hilton become apparent. The changes that initially met with resistance eventually led to improvements that were recognized and appreciated. This realization helped the company bridge the gap and adapt to new challenges, proving that change, when managed thoughtfully, could enhance stability and growth.

This holistic approach helped me navigate the complexities of organizational change at Hilton, overcoming initial rejections by fostering collaboration, building trust, and always showing respect for the foundations laid by those who had come before me.

As I've said many times, it's a people-oriented business. If you're not a people person, with the patience to listen, you won't get far.

Juggling so many regions and cultures in one job was another challenge. IHG had trained me well. You learn to be agile and flexible. A colleague remarked, "I think you're successful because of your adaptability. You can joke around with a bellman and then hold court in front of kings and queens."

I mentioned al-Masudi before: he succeeded as a scholar because he could move from culture to culture with ease (at a time when international travel was difficult and perilous), and he spoke to people of all stripes. I operated in the same fashion, navigating cultural differences with ease, like a chameleon: blending in to whatever environment I found myself in. I can be Jewish with the Jews, Muslim with the Muslims, and Christian with the Christians.

It was fascinating to observe how culture impacted work. In Eastern Europe, business is very transactional, formal, and unemotional. If you're negotiating a deal, you eschew hours of wining and dining for straight talk: let's just meet in the office and work out the details.

An exception is in Russia, where business is also conducted in blunt, transactional fashion but where, if you *do* find yourself dining with an associate or business partner, all bets are off. Prepare for a marathon session of eating and drinking, replete with many courses, dishes of smoked and pickled fish, caviar, hearty dumplings, meat and poultry, steaming platters of buckwheat, and a lot of vodka (including the accompanying toasts.)

I learned that Russians either love you or hate you. If they love you, you've got their business forever. If not, well, you might as well take the first taxi back to Sheremetyevo Airport.

In Turkey and the Gulf states, there is a more collegial, roundabout way to doing business. A friendly rapport must be established before any deals are signed. That means a lot of lunches, teas, coffees, casual chats, exchanging of greetings and small gifts during the holidays, and so forth. It's more relationship-driven and requires a lot of face time.

Work ethic and workplace culture also vary widely. In the south of France or parts of Italy, if an employee, even a manager, takes a vacation for the entirety of August, no one would bat an eye (and they'd probably think it odd if you were answering work emails while on holiday!). In Nigeria, you might not have a job when you returned on September 1st!

Being a chameleon also requires you to avoid painting whole countries or regions with a broad brush. For example, if you're overseeing Southeast Asia, that includes Indonesia, Thailand, the Philippines, Singapore, and East Timor, among others. Sure, these countries have some commonalities, but each has its own history, identity, and way of life. Or take the Middle East: there is a vast gulf—in both senses of the word—between Saudi Arabia and Lebanon. Geography might put different countries in the same room, but it's far from an absolute equalizer.

My success in the role was dependent on keeping track of what was going on in the field while remaining part and parcel of the corporate structure. A lot of companies like to brand themselves as "global in structure but local in outlook." But it's usually not true—for the most part, the leadership is oblivious to what is happening on the ground. You need to pick the right leaders who can interface between the global/corporate level and the local level. Most companies, not just in hospitality but in general, don't get it right. Or they don't allow regional business units enough autonomy to operate and make decisions.

The business of hospitality works best when people, functions, and processes are interwoven and interdependent. I learned this lesson my first day on the job as a lowly dishwasher. No one gives the dishwasher much regard, but if he doesn't show up to work, guess what? You're not serving dinner that night. Unless you want your guests eating off paper plates. This illustrates how one disruption can grind the whole operation to a halt.

Housekeeping is dependent on laundry. You can tidy up a room but without fresh sheets and towels, no one is sleeping there. And, of course, front office reception depends on both. And sales cannot function without all of those functions working together in tandem.

Hospitality encompasses almost every other function under one roof. When you step up to corporate you have multiple disciplines: legal, development, finance, revenue management, design and engineering, hotel opening teams, IT, operations. Just like in an individual hotel, they're all interdependent and all dictate the success of the company.

In the last 20 years, hospitality has become more "matrixed" at the corporate level, where there is a lot less coordination between units. The realities of geography and spatial dispersal adds to the challenge: you could be living in Dubai while your boss is in London. Sometimes this lack of supervision exacerbates the siloed, fragmented structure. Unless you have a leader who knows how to work the matrix and can pull people together, based on a common goal, the organization will suffer.

That was also something I had to deal with—and something I still grapple with in my current role. The leader must be able to pull people together and build bridges—to make people feel part of an ecosystem, even if their direct line manager isn't sitting next to them.

Ultimately, I am proud of what I achieved as a VP at Hilton. We built one of the best performing sales and marketing organizations in the industry, aligned operational objectives with commercial objectives, and opened sales offices in key countries (which continue to operate to this day). When I left, the department's sales team had grown to 240 members working across 136 hotels in operation with more than 90 new properties in the pipeline.

Finally, the gremlin had been defeated, never to surface again.

CHAPTER 7

AIRLINES, ZIPLINES, BOTTOM LINES, AND ADRENALINE

Since the first humans looked up with envy at the birds in the sky, our species has coveted the gift of flight.

In 2018, I gave that gift to the little-known emirate of Ras Al-Khaimah.

You can experience it yourself if you come visit. First, you travel upward, 1,500 meters above sea level, through the Hajar Mountains, an otherworldly landscape of rocky crags and lush oases.

At the site, you carefully approach the ledge from which you will launch yourself and take a deep breath. Don't look down (or maybe do): you're hundreds of feet above the stone mountain *wadis*, beneath bright blue skies and a burning sun, unless you chose to visit during the winter season, where the sun rays are softer and the breeze is cooler. The austere beauty of Jebel Jais, the UAE's tallest mountain, spreads before you. You take one last look at this stunning vista, say a quick prayer, and step off into the void.

Next thing you know you're flying at 90 miles per hour (150 km/hour), a speed that puts even the birds to shame. For the next two to three minutes, you can feel what it's like to have wings.

This is the pulse-quickening experience of the Jebel Jais Zipline, the longest zipline in the world, and one that I had more than just a hand in building.

So, how did I go from handling an outbound marketing strategy in Moscow to building attractions for adrenaline junkies from the United Arab Emirates and around the world? I'll tell you.

A BRUSH WITH ROYALTY

In 2013, the Hilton executive team and I took part in the opening of the Waldorf Astoria in Ras al-Khaimah, where I met His Highness Sheikh Saud bin Saqr Al Qasimi, the ruler of the emirate and, at the time, the direct owner of the hotel. The UAE, in case you didn't know, is a federation of seven emirates, each ruled by a Sheikh. He's a monarch, so people tend to get nervous around him. But I found His Highness to be humble, charming and approachable.

I introduced myself, and His Highness was intrigued by my name.

"Where are you from?" he asked. "You might be Arab, but your name is very Bedouin," referring to the semi-nomadic people that have populated North Africa and the Middle East for centuries.

He called over another man, by the name of Abdullah Mattar. "Abdullah, come meet Haitham! This guy is your cousin!" His Highness chuckled.

Abdullah was from a village in RAK called Digdagga. A place known for its cattle that produce rich, fresh milk, which you can only buy locally. They don't export it, even to the other emirates.

Fast forward two years. I get a call from an Anglo-Indian gentleman who worked for His Highness telling me he wanted to meet me at his palace.

I figured he wanted to discuss the performance of Hilton's portfolio. Back then Hilton had seven of the total ten or 11 hotels in the emirate. People across the UAE used to refer to RAK as Hilton Island. In any event, when a monarch summons you to his palace, you don't say no!

The grounds of the palace were lush and verdant, replete with peacocks roaming free and very vocal birds. Inside, I was ushered into a richly appointed "*majlis*," a traditional Arabic sitting room where guests are received, and business is conducted.

His Highness greeted me warmly. But he wasn't interested in talking profits and projections; the conversation was more low-key. We spent a couple of hours getting to know each other. He asked about my own education, my kids, and where they had attended school.

Pleasantries observed, the real purpose of the meeting was soon revealed: he proposed that I head up the emirate's new tourism board. The UAE had long been a major tourist destination for the Middle East region and the world at large. Dubai was, and remains, its crown jewel, attracting, at the time, around 15 million tourists annually. The capital city of Abu Dhabi was the #2 destination. But Ras al-Khaimah had long been overlooked by both domestic and international travelers. His Highness had a clear vision for his emirate and he wanted to see it realized.

At the time RAK received close to 300,000 tourists each year. The goal was to multiply that by ten. And to do it within a decade.

I was honored, but I told him, "I've never worked in tourism."

"How many hotels are you managing?" he asked.

"One hundred and thirty-five."

"In the whole of RAK, we have only 25 hotels. I'm confident you can handle the job."

It was an intriguing offer. But I didn't accept right off the bat. I had a few conditions. First, I told him I didn't want to be beholden to a board or report to anyone but His Highness for the first six months. I knew that if I was going to run an operation like that, it would work best if I had a mandate to do my thing without a lot of bureaucracy or pre-existing processes. I just needed a free hand to make things happen and make them happen fast.

Second, I asked for a research budget so we could collect our own data instead of relying on third party data. To me this was critical to forming a destination strategy. In business and government realms, broadly speaking, strategies tend to be worth no more than the paper they're printed on. Simply because most leaders don't act on them. They sit on a shelf collecting dust. I was determined to execute on the vision we came up with, and I needed reliable, objective data to make it happen.

As they say, a destination without a strategy is a recipe for disaster.

On the second point, he agreed willingly. On the first, he said, "That is acceptable, but if you're reporting directly to me, that makes you a kind of de facto minister."

I didn't want to be a minister, but I did want a free hand to run things the way I envisioned, and to be able to accelerate progress without the brakes of bureaucracy. His Highness didn't like bureaucracy either, but some of the people around him were more considered and cautious in their approach.

I was duly appointed by "emiri decree," and granted official authority. This was quite a change from everything I had done before. As a vice president in the corporate hierarchy, I had decision making powers, but this was the first time I had government-backed authority to do almost anything for the benefit of the emirate and its people.

The key to power is how you channel it. Time would tell how I would use mine.

LEARNING THE ROPES

My position also brought me into the fold of the United Nations World Tourism Organization (UNWTO, now called UN Tourism). The agency's core purpose is to promote responsible, sustainable tourism and find ways to make the industry friendlier to people and planet alike. It offers leadership support to both developed and developing nations, driving tourism to be a force that stimulates economic growth.

I wasn't an official government minister, but I was doing the work of one and was recognized by the UNWTO as such. I attended ministerial roundtables, summits, and conferences, where I had the privilege of listening to government officials from 180 states discussing the industry, globally and locally: challenges, opportunities, the investment landscape, social issues such as environmental impact and over tourism, ways of developing the sector, etc. To me this was the most educational part of my career, learning from experts and changemakers.

I served on the committee that drafted the 2017 UNWTO "Sustainable Development Goals," which is the guidebook for sustainable tourism development worldwide. Today, I'm still special adviser to Zurab Pololikashvili, Secretary General of the UNWTO.

During these summits, I took copious notes, asked questions, and wasn't shy about introducing myself to people, including important ministers. In a single afternoon I'd pick the brain of leaders from Italy or Kenya or Spain. How is your ministry structured? What does governance look like? What bilateral agreements do you have? How do you collaborate with other states?

This way I learned the trade and started figuring out how we could establish a tourist framework in RAK.

Back home, I sat down with His Highness in his palace. I said, "Your Highness, we're not Spain. They get 90 million tourists a year. But this is how they've done it." No need to reinvent the wheel—study what others have done well and adapt it to your own jurisdiction. If it can work in a vast and complex tourism sector like Spain, it could probably work for us.

We were laying the groundwork, but we wanted a tangible, opening-shot kind of victory to show we were making progress.

I had begun hosting various events in the emirate to help put us on the map, but nothing major had taken place.

For 13 years, the Arabian Hotel Investment Conference (AHIC), now known as the Future Hospitality Summit, a significant hospitality summit attended by investors, thought leaders, hotel operators, architects, and other stakeholders, had taken place in Dubai.

That year, I gave a speech at the convention in Dubai, and when I came off the stage, I was greeted by the chairman of The Bench, which was the founding organization of AHIC. He said he liked what I said and expressed an interest in having me return.

"I'd love that, but I'd love to do it in Ras Al-Khaimah."

He didn't immediately take to the idea. As I said, RAK was kind of the overlooked younger sibling to Dubai and Abu Dhabi. It was a tough sell.

He had never even been to RAK, so I invited him and his team to visit the opulent Waldorf Astoria RAK, and took them on a junket to showcase the best of the emirate. Jonathan was impressed by its natural beauty, stunning beaches and majestic mountains. The marine life and wildlife had the same effect.

I tried pitching the idea of hosting the conference again. We could put everyone up at the Waldorf and build an amazing temporary conference facility right on the beach. I sweetened the offer by promising that he could design the conference space he wanted. It's every conference organizer's dream. The venue was the biggest selling point.

The next year, I beamed with pride when AHIC convened at the Waldorf in RAK. It was a victory on two fronts. We not only had to convince the organizers to move it there, we had to convince foreign investors, hoteliers, and other attendees to skip Dubai and come to an unfamiliar part of the Emirates. But evidently, it worked. The conference rooms were thronged with the industry's best and brightest, from all over the EMEA region, some dressed in dark, pressed suits, others more casual, and some attendees from the Gulf wearing the traditional dress, black or soft colored *abaya* for women, and all-white *thobe* for men.

That year, we set the AHIC record for number of attendees, totaling more than a thousand, including many motivated investors who ended up purchasing land in the emirate on Al Marjan, a 'reclaimed island.' At first it was designated for residential use, but I asked His Highness to allow us to remaster the plan and change the zoning to permit hotel development. We needed more hotel rooms to be able to accommodate the anticipated growth in tourism. So AHIC was a symbolic, as well as a practical, victory for us.

This landmark event helped put RAK on the world map for insiders in the hotel business, opening the floodgates for additional summits, roundtables, conventions, and other infrastructure-building events.

Meanwhile, I worked with His Highness to introduce a tourism tax on hotels. The hotels didn't complain because they could expect higher revenues once we rolled out our plan (and typically such taxes are passed on to the consumer, who doesn't mind paying the equivalent of a few dollars a night extra.) Those taxes went directly back into our own fund, which we then reinvested into our destination development efforts.

That was the first phase of the mission. But obviously, all that tourist infrastructure isn't created for nothing. You still need tourists!

We turned our focus to what visitors want. That's Business 101: listen to what the market demands and build a narrative around that. We conducted surveys in what we identified as potential key feeder markets, which helped us zero in on what people were looking for.

What was our brand identity? RAK isn't Paris, Rome, or Dubai. We're a small emirate and can't compete with the top destinations by trying to emulate them, or being something we're not. We had to work with what we had.

What were our demand generators? Why do people travel and why would they come? We identified three categories of attractions: 1) the classic "beach, sun, and sand" vibe that perennially lures tourists to warm climates; 2) culture, heritage, and historical sites, and 3) outdoor adventure.

We definitely had beaches, many of which are more pristine and less crowded than in more populous parts of the UAE. And the coastal waters teem with stunning marine life. There's a fish market where the fishermen sell their catch around dawn. You can buy it there, have it cleaned, and the chef at your hotel will cook it for you to order.

We had a rich and little-known cultural and historical patrimony going back 7,000 years, to the Bronze Age. As a trade center at the crossroads of several different ancient civilizations, RAK's history and archaeological heritage is deep. You can see castles and forts that have stood the test of time, like the palace of the Queen of Sheba. Not to mention the UAE's oldest village, built from coral stones, Jazeera Al Hamra.

We also had striking natural landscapes, including the highest mountain range, and a beautiful terracotta desert, that could appeal to outdoorsy types and adventure-seekers. You can climb a mountain peak and swim in the Arabian Gulf in one afternoon.

We did a survey to see how many people in the UAE even knew RAK had a mountain, much less the highest. Only 10% even knew about it, and certainly didn't know it by name.

We "branded" the mountain and gave it its own logo. Then we commissioned the building of the first ever viewing deck on the mountain, with dramatic vistas of the rocky mountains and the shimmering sea. We created a new café and restaurant onsite, called Puro, which my team and I developed conceptually. Then we added campsites, so people could turn their day trip into an overnight stay.

It was a good start. But I felt we needed something more, something *big*, some unique attraction that would generate buzz and draw people from faraway lands.

That's when the idea of a zipline came up. It seemed like the right place for it, with the dramatic vistas of the desert and mountains.

None of us knew the first thing about ziplines, so we got to work. I learned that the longest zipline in the world, the Guinness record holder, was in Puerto Rico's Toro Verde, a park owned by two Costa Rican developers, George and Ricardo.

In a few weeks, I was flying out to Puerto Rico with one of my team members, to meet with Ricardo, George and the minister of tourism there. They greeted us with a chauffeured car, complete with a fixer, and took me to the zipline. I rode it myself and it was every bit as thrilling as promised. As soon as I finished, breathless with excitement, I thought, "We need this in RAK."

I sat down to talk business with George and Ricardo, who were proud of what they had built, an awesome tourist attraction with a flawless safety record.

I said, "I'm going to build the longest zipline in the world." "Ours is already the longest."

"I know. I'm going to build an even longer one."

"You're not doing it without us!" they said.

We worked out a deal and, in a few months, they arrived to start surveying the mountains for the perfect location, in preparation for construction of the Jebel Jais zipline. Even before it opened, the project garnered a lot of global press. When it was completed, it was, as promised, a marvel of engineering, spanning a greater distance than any zipline ever built. It uses no motors or engines or electricity; it's powered purely by your own body weight.

That mighty mountain had sat there for eons, an untapped tourist resource. In a few short years we turned it into a gold mine. And we didn't need to be "another Dubai." We just had to leverage what we already had on our own turf.

Meanwhile, RAK was building new hotels, luring international hotel brands, and boosting the emirate's profile. We also provided local workers English language training so they could better serve the influx of tourists from abroad. I went on road shows and trade shows, introducing RAK to the rest of the world.

My strength was Eastern Europe, which I already knew intimately from my work at Hilton. Dubai attracts 15 million tourists a year, which means they don't need to advertise to smaller markets such as Central or Eastern Europe. But just as I had done at Hilton, I recognized the potential there: small but growing countries with a consumer base that loved to travel, could reach the UAE in five or six hours, and sought beaches, outdoor excursions, and adventure in warm climates, especially in fall and winter. Fifteen million visitors is a big pie; I just needed to slice off a small piece to achieve success.

When I joined, RAK's visitors were 70% domestic tourists, 30% international. We wanted to boost the number of visitors from abroad and reverse those figures. Foreigners tend to do more and spend more, whereas the domestic market tended to visit only during weekends and public holidays. They also tended to stick around the resorts and not venture outside. The international tourists usually stay longer, spend more, and prefer to leave the resort to explore the destination and its offerings. We needed hotels to be full Monday through Friday too.

In time, thanks to our aggressive marketing, we brought in more international visitors, and flipped the ratio, to 70/30 in favor of those abroad.

My next mission was to cut a deal with Emirates, one of the UAE's two flag carriers, to further encourage inbound tourists to come visit us. Ras Al Khaimah has its own international airport, but it's small, with limited capacity and mainly services low-cost airlines or chartered flights. RAK is only 45 minutes by car from Dubai, so it didn't really make sense to try to redirect flights to our own emirate. But perhaps I could work out some other kind of deal with the airline.

I started a dialogue with the Chief Commercial Officer of Emirates Airline, a Frenchman with a very strong accent named Thierry.

He said, "I can't do anything for you. You need the chief of tourism in Dubai to approve that."

I reached out to the chief of Dubai Tourism, and we met in his office. He and I knew each other well from my Hilton days, as I had sat on his Dubai Hotels Executive Board. "Your Excellency, I need your help. Ras al Khaimah is Dubai's little brother. We're not trying to step on anyone's toes, but I need your help with Emirates. I want to bring foreign tourists to RAK Airport on Emirates."

"How do you plan to do that?"

"I plan to package deals with tour operators and travelers in Eastern Europe. A five-night package, two nights in Dubai and three in RAK," I said.

"Not a bad idea. But who's going to pay for the marketing?"

"We will."

"You have the funds?"

"Yes."

"Ok. You've got my approval. Our office is representing Dubai but we're all one nation. Tell Thierry."

"I'm not leaving until you call them yourself!" I said.

He laughed, then called up Emirates and said "Haitham is our brother, we want to help him make this deal."

When you book business class with Emirates, they'll pick you up in a nice BMW, marked Business Class, to take you to and from your hotel, your home or your office. So, the first time I started seeing their branded BMW taking passengers from Dubai to RAK hotels, I was over the moon. I even took pictures!

More deals followed as Emirates launched new routes from other Central and Eastern European destinations. I smiled from ear to ear when I boarded the inaugural flight from Dubai to Zagreb.

By 2019, we hit 1.2 million annual tourists, an astounding increase from the 300,000 where we began. The fledgling staff of five people when I came in ballooned to 130, and tourism tax revenues quadrupled.

Today, RAK tourism is thriving. We won't steal the spotlight from flashier destinations like Dubai or Abu Dhabi, but that was never our mission. All we wanted was to enable the people of RAK to share in the wealth generated by the tourism industry, and to show Emiratis, and the world, that our little corner of the Arabian Peninsula, inhabited for seven millennia, had a lot to offer. And I see that the benefit of this growth is widespread: everyone from the vendors in the Kuwaiti Souq in RAK, to the guy on the roadside selling homemade honey, to owners of luxury hotels and restaurants, are cashing in.

ACROSS THE GULF

Opportunity begets opportunity.

At a UNWTO conference in St. Petersburg, Russia, where I gave a talk in 2019, I was honored to be seated next to the new Saudi Minister of Tourism at dinner, where we got to know each other.

"I've heard a lot about you," he told me. He was familiar with my work at the UN and my achievements boosting tourism in RAK with a small marketing fund.

A few weeks later, I got a call from his office. They had hired an outside firm to develop a tourism strategy and they wanted to hire me alongside a couple of other industry experts, to assess the firm's work. I accepted an invitation to meet with them in London.

I declined their offer to pay me a day rate, saying it would be enough for me to be involved in this unique opportunity and they were generous enough and covered travel expenses. But I had to clear it with my own boss. His Highness, the ruler, said "All the Arab countries are one country. Their success is our success. So go."

For the next four days I lived and worked at the Four Seasons Hotel in Hampshire, a beautiful 18th century Georgian manor house that sits on 500 acres of pristine English countryside, replete with a gently flowing river and grazing horses.

I was an active participant and challenged the consultant company on some of their assumptions, numbers, and targets. At the end of three days, His Excellency said "I need to meet with my team privately. The consultants can stay in the room."

When I didn't follow them into the adjoining chamber, His Excellency grabbed me from the hallway. "What are you doing here? You should come inside with us. You're one of our team."

So, I went in the room and he said, "We were impressed with your work, your candor, your professionalism. We felt you were one of us. We'd like you to join us." I'd be a senior adviser to the ministry and help develop what was then the Saudi Tourism Commission into an official ministry.

I said I was open to the idea. But this was a big step up.

Comparatively speaking, RAK is a small village of 400,000 people. Saudi Arabia is a massive, politically and culturally important nation of 36 million, with a mega tourism budget.

The country draws around 20 million international tourists each year, so it wasn't exactly a hidden gem. But there was room for growth. Also, most of those visitors came for religious pilgrimages, and the government was interested in developing other sectors of the tourist market.

I resigned from RAK and joined the Saudi team in September 2019.

As it turned out, I had a lot to learn about Saudi Arabia. As is often the case, there is more than meets the eye. I was surprised, for example, to learn that one of the hottest countries on the planet experiences snowfall, up in Jabal Al Lawz (the Mountain of Almonds.) Saudi has the largest olive farm in al Jawf and UNESCO heritage date farm in Al

Ahsa. And a litany of agricultural, archaeological, cultural, and historical sites.

One memorable curiosity was the village of Jubbah in Ha'il, one of the oldest settlements of the kingdom. Such is its tradition of extreme generosity, and hospitality, there are no doors on the houses. As if to say, "Come, traveler, enter and have some coffee and dates."

Jeddah, where I conducted most of my business, is known as the bride's pearl—the bride being the Red Sea. Jeddah has always been a port city, which has contributed to its more relaxed, liberal nature compared to elsewhere in the kingdom. Jeddans are fond of saying "Jeddah ghair," meaning Jeddah is just different.

BAGGAGE ALLOWANCE

My mission in Saudi Arabia was similar to my previous one, albeit on a much larger scale: build a self-sustaining tourist infrastructure and boost tourist numbers, especially from overseas.

For 200 years, Saudi Arabia was mostly isolated and closed off. Yes, there were foreign visitors, guest workers, and expats, but for the most part, the country resisted modernity and was set in its ways. Now it was opening up.

In Ras al-Khaimah, we were basically starting with a clean slate. No one, even Emiratis, knew much about the emirate, so we could brand it as we wished.

However, Saudi Arabia's reputation preceded it—it came with a lot of "baggage." In the West, when people think of Saudi Arabia, they picture a land of minarets, sand, oil, and *abayas*. It is associated with strictness, piety, and inhibition—not the first place that comes to mind as a leisure travel destination. To put it mildly, Saudi Arabia had a less than stellar image in the West.

A huge part of our mission was changing perceptions to say that Saudi is not the country you think it is. It's more than that. Yes, it's not a freewheeling party destination like Amsterdam or Berlin. But neither is it a place where you can't let your hair down (women too) and have fun. For a foreign tourist, it's a place where you can relax, dress normally, go to concerts and be accepted.

First, I had to put together a team, basically from scratch. Nearly a third of the population of Saudi Arabia is made up of expatriates who power its industries and provide both high-skill and low-skill labor. But that wasn't for us: we were "Saudi-zing", localizing the tourism workforce. Given the sector had taken a backseat to other fields, Saudis weren't too familiar with tourism as a profession. Luckily, we had the benefit of an educated pool of talent, especially younger Saudis who have traveled overseas and wanted to be plugged into a world beyond their borders. What they lacked in experience they made up for in willingness to learn.

Generally speaking, Saudis are well travelled and are used to being served; serving others, which is the essence of hospitality, is somewhat unfamiliar to them. So, this was also something that our new recruits had to learn. It didn't come naturally, and it took some effort to convey that, "You're now the host, not the guest." But they adapted fast.

While the workforce was primarily Saudi, I did strategically supplement local talent with international recruits. It just made sense when you had to serve various markets abroad. For example, if you want to attract tourists from China, it's prudent to bring in a Chinese national who speaks the language, knows the market, and has local connections. We opted for specialists in charge of outbound markets in the UK, US, and Europe.

So, now we had thrown open the doors of the Saudi kingdom and put a team on the ground. What next? Saudi Arabia boasts good infrastructure (roads, highways, seaports, airports). What it lacked was tourism infrastructure. We had the attractions, but how do you ferry tourists around from site to site? Where will they stay? Who will serve as their tour guide in a country where English is not widely spoken?

You have to create a whole ecosystem of investors, service providers (destination management companies or DMCs, hotel operators, tour companies), government officials overseeing tourism, and of course consumers (the tourists themselves.) It has to be profitable for the people involved and make good business sense in order to take root and grow.

We had to find DMCs or tour operators. We had only two or three small companies who were limited to taking groups of around 20 people on tours at a time. And our goal was a hundred million total visitors by 2023. In the whole country there were 150 tour guides and only two could speak good English.

We negotiated incentives from the government to encourage investment and created a guidebook for the private sector to develop its capacity. This brought me into contact with some heavy hitters, such as a billionaire entrepreneur from India and deep-pocketed tour company owners. I also leveraged my connections with folks in the travel industry and in government, including in other ministries, such as the Ministry of Culture and Ministry of Investment.

Just as things were getting off the ground, a microscopic virus in Wuhan, China, had other plans for us.

I don't need to repeat the story of the emergence of COVID-19, because if you were alive when it happened, you remember vividly how quickly the dominoes fell once it spread beyond Asia. Almost overnight, everything ground to a halt. Global travel was no exception. Hotels locked up, airlines reduced their flight schedules, and nations dropped the drawbridge, saying no to foreign visitors. Saudi Arabia was closed entirely, and restrictions were imposed on who could enter. In 2020, the *hajj* pilgrimage to Mecca, which normally draws between one and two million people, was reduced, for the first time in 1,500 years, to 10,000 socially distanced worshipers from Saudi and the Gulf countries only.

Obviously COVID was devastating for hospitality and tourism. But in our case, to Saudi's Tourism Ministry, in its nascent state, it was kind of a blessing in disguise. We could put things on pause and continue our internal development work at a slower pace without having to worry about incoming tourists, when we were not totally ready to host them. If not for the virus, running our campaign would have been like trying to refuel, clean and restock a plane in mid-flight.

By August 2020, the Saudi government relaxed COVID restrictions to allow for domestic tourism. It was summer, so we launched a campaign touting the cooler areas of Saudi, the likes of Abha and Al Baha areas—educating Saudis about their own country. Saudis prefer traveling abroad, where there is more entertainment and fewer restrictions. But the attractions we had opened, and were actively marketing, sparked interest from Saudi nationals. Social media was abuzz with comments like, "Wait, that's in *our* country? We have green mountains and *snow?*"

The novelty of snow in the Gulf inspired another fun ad campaign. I thought, let's not just talk about it, let's show it in all its wintery wonder. So, in the winter, we commissioned an ad featuring people frolicking in the snow. We imported a sleigh from Italy and hired models from Lebanon, France, and Italy. When I pitched it to the minister, his eyes lit up. "I love it...do you think we can get camels up there in the photo shoot?"

I said "Let's see what we can do." Camels aren't usually present on Jebel Al Lawz, where the snowfall happens every year, but we orchestrated their transport up to the mountain.

It was probably one of the few times in human history camels have been photographed next to a sleigh and people skiing!

Tourism is branding. People pick a destination because they associate it with a certain experience. In Italy it's pizza, pasta, and winding medieval streets. In Japan it's taking in the duality of temples, kimonos, and graceful cherry trees alongside neon lights, mega-cities, and crazy fashion. Every destination has a brand.

In Saudi, we were changing that brand, that image. I said, "Look, Saudi is more than sand and sun. We have lush green mountains, beautiful untouched beaches and amazing historical sites. We also have winter! It's a big, vast and incredibly diverse country that is much more than meets the eye. Come see it for yourself."

The ad campaign generated positive responses at home and abroad and also boosted my team's confidence. They saw that with a vision, an expanded concept of what's possible, and a bit of creativity, we really could put Saudi Arabia on the tourist map.

It also scored points for me as someone who was still trying to prove that a foreigner imported from the "village" of RAK could succeed in a much bigger, more challenging market.

My firm belief is, whether you're promoting a small emirate or a vast county, the fundamentals are the same. Give people what they want, even if they don't yet know what they want, and make it easier for them to experience it once they arrive.

Indulge their imagination. Intrigue them. Inspire them to explore and engage with the destination and all it has to offer.

CHAPTER 8

TIME IS A SWORD

This chapter is different from the rest of the book. It's not about hospitality or tourism per se. It's a story about something we all face: the unalterable reality that time marches on. It's a cautionary tale that ambition and striving must not get the better of you, and a reminder that work is a means to an end, not an end unto itself. Even for people, like me, who love their work.

It's an important lesson, because if you forget it, your life can fly by in the blink of an eye. In some cases, forgetting can be fatal.

My friend Jochem-Jan Sleiffer—whom everyone knew as JJ— was a tall, silver-haired Dutchman with a big smile and a bigger personality. When I first met him in 2011, he was VP of Operations for Western Europe at Hilton. We served on an executive committee together for the Europe/ Middle East/Africa region. This committee convened a few times a year. During those conferences, JJ and I got to know each other over coffee breaks, team lunches and at the gym every morning. Over time, these work chats blossomed into a friendship. We were from very different backgrounds, but we had a few fundamental things in common. For example, he also started at an entry level position in the kitchen and worked his way up. We had both been through the trenches. Among the many things I liked about JJ, he, like me, never forgot where he came from.

I also liked that he was honest, straightforward and trustworthy – admirable qualities, shared by many of his countrymen.

When I left Hilton for the RAK tourism board in 2015, we kind of lost touch. I mean, we stayed friends, but we didn't speak often. Later, as you know, I started working for the Saudi tourism ministry, so I frequently made the jump across the Gulf between the UAE and Saudi Arabia.

By that time, JJ had been promoted to Hilton's president for the Middle East, Africa, and Turkey, and, while he was still based in Dubai, business often took him to Saudi Arabia. When our plans converged, whether in Riyadh, Jeddah, Dubai or some other destination, we took advantage of the opportunity to meet. It's one thing to get together with a friend in your hometown, but meeting abroad adds a special element, and deepens the bond. I also helped JJ out by introducing him to key Saudi government officials I knew through my own network.

The corporate environment can be cutthroat, so hanging out with JJ was a breath of fresh air. He was pleasant, positive, energetic, and rarely complained. Back home in Dubai, we also hung out regularly. We were both indoor cycling enthusiasts at CRANK, which is like SoulCycle in America, and we attended classes a couple of times a week, whenever JJ or I were not travelling.

He'd always give me a hard time about my cycling scores.

"Hey old man, you're too slow, pick up the pace!" he would say.

"You're not faster than me, you've just got longer legs," I would reply. At 6'2", he did have a natural advantage.

Spin classes are invigorating, a lot more than you'd expect from riding a stationary bike in a gym. You feed off the energy of the instructor, the camaraderie and friendly competition of your fellow riders, the music, the sweat, the desire to push yourself. That's something I had always relished since I was a teenager: pushing yourself, even when it's hard. *Especially* when it's hard. All my life I had done that professionally; now I found an outlet to do it physically.

After several years in tourism, I had started to miss working in hospitality. So, when IHG's COO Pascal told me he was retiring, I leaped at the chance to take over. It was basically a dream job: I would be chief executive of an entire region, something I had long wanted.

I asked Pascal to tell the hiring committee to add my name to the list of candidates. Then I waited patiently. But a few weeks later Pascal told me "I don't think it's gonna be your turn. They're going with a lady in APAC," meaning the Asia-Pacific region.

I was disappointed but accepted it. It wasn't meant to be.

But ten months later, Pascall called me again. "I've got some news for you, Haitham. The candidate in Asia has declined the move for personal reasons and can't accept the role. Do you still wish to be considered?"

"Absolutely," I said.

That prompted a rush of interviews with high level people at IHG. As a former executive-level employee at the company and a government official for the past seven years, you'd think I'd be able to bypass at least some of the background check. Nope! They scrutinized my history and combed through my background as if I was applying to run the CIA! They looked at criminal records in every country I had worked in, and I was subjected to various aptitude tests, which took hours, along with a psychometric survey. I also had to meet with an employment psychologist, who analyzed me through and through before giving me a "recommended."

It was intense and rigorous. It dragged on for four months. I was competing with four other candidates. I didn't know who they were and resisted the urge to ask, lest I start comparing myself to them. It wouldn't have done any good. I just tried to be the best I could be.

As time went on the other candidates dropped from four to three to two.

In April 2021, I got a call in the morning from London, from Kenneth, the CEO of the region. "Haitham," he said, "it's gonna be you."

I was elated. That night I celebrated with my wife and children. It was by far the biggest career milestone to date, and the fulfillment of a years-long dream.

When I reported for work on my first day in the new role, there was a rush of nostalgia. You know the feeling when you return to a familiar place, with some familiar faces, after eleven years: a weird combination of "old" and "new." Everything is mostly the same, but little things were different. Some folks remained from my earlier tenure, but there were a lot of new faces.

I took over the old COO's office, in the corner, where I had only been allowed in when my predecessor would summon me. That's the office I still occupy today. From my windows, I can see the shimmering Gulf, and gaze at the majestic skyscrapers that are a symbol of Dubai's modernity and prosperity. If I look closely, I can spot in the distance the old house where I once lived and the first hotel I worked in. The InterContinental Dubai, the legacy hotel that started it all back in 1975.

My first days on the job, I mused about how much Dubai had changed since I arrived, and how much I had changed with it. And I recalled the people I once knew, who had shaped my career, one way or the other. Like John, whom I once told, "One day, I'm going to have your job."

John is long gone. But I'm still here. My proclamation had come true.

But the celebratory verve I felt quickly cooled in the face of new challenges.

IHG had been known in the region as the sleeping giant – a great company with unfulfilled potential. There was immense work to do. I came in guns blazing, ready to deploy a 90-day plan like a general implementing a battle strategy.

My goal was: make a measurable impact in year one, in trading, growth, guest satisfaction, everything. But I only assumed the position in April, right at the end of the pandemic, so we really only had seven months to do a year's worth of work.

First, I wanted to repair and reestablish important relationships (e.g. with some hotel owners) that had deteriorated. I reached out to those owners and said, "I am at your service." Just hearing it caught them by surprise; they had grown accustomed to a more indifferent style of leadership. But that had to change.

Of the eleven people in my leadership team, about half were on board with my ambitious plans. The other half dug their heels in. It was the tail end of COVID and they had gotten accustomed to a more relaxed way of doing things.

A few people quit. They felt it was all too much. I respected that. It was in the interest of both parties to part ways. We had to terminate a few other folks, an unfortunate task, but necessary.

So, already we had a 50% turnover in the leadership team, which intensified the pressure to meet our End of Year goals.

Meanwhile, I was readjusting to the work culture of IHG, which evidently deserved its "sleeping giant" (in the Middle East, at least) moniker for more reasons than one. One of the company's pillars was "move fast," but I had joined one of the slowest companies on earth. Just to get something simple done involved a lot of hoop-jumping, multiple approval layers and endless opinion-soliciting from various people. It was very bureaucratic and "matrixed," and much of that was beyond my control.

As the months wore on, my team members and I were under a great deal of stress as we worked tirelessly to meet our goals. I started getting calls from the company's HR that some people had complained I was too hard on them.

I was sympathetic, but I said, "If you want performance, that's the only way. You're going to have to trust me. You hired me from a shortlist of top candidates. You've done your due diligence. Just let me do the job for you and I'll do it right."

They said, "Okay, we trust you."

Well, sure enough, when December came around, we had not just met, but exceeded our benchmarks, achieving amazing results in profitability, trading, revenues, growth and market share.

During a well-deserved celebration with the team, I said, "What we did was exceptional. We proved we could do something in seven months what others hadn't done in years. Who thinks we can do it again next year?'

Everyone raised their hands.

I promised I'd provide whatever they needed to make it possible and let them get on with their jobs. But repeating those results next year would mean we'd have to stretch ourselves again.

In May 2022, I flew to Washington DC for my daughter's graduation from George Washington University. I try to get a workout in, even on the road—when you travel as much as I do, it's essential—so I found a SoulCycle a few blocks from my hotel.

But during the class, something strange happened. My body recoiled at the exertion. I was wheezing and felt weirdly fatigued. In Dubai I cycled two or three times each week, and nothing like that had ever happened.

I figured the feeling would dissipate once I got off the bike, but even walking back to the hotel, I was short of breath. Something was very wrong.

Immediately, I called my doctor in Dubai. He reassured me that I was in great health. Just a few months prior, he did a full health checkup (something I do annually). Everything was intact.

Despite his lack of concern, I insisted on seeing him as soon as I got back to Dubai, one week later. They ran a battery of tests on me, and he came back with a disconcerting revelation: they had detected an abnormality and said they'd have to do an angiogram, which is a close study of the veins and arteries.

"Study" is an understatement. It's basically a surgical procedure. They knock you out. When I woke up, the doctor said "I have bad news. You've got clogged arteries. It's very serious." It was, he said, one of the gravest cases he had seen.

"Sometimes the heart creates an extra blood vessel to make up for a blockage; yours has made four. In my 20-year medical career I've never seen this happen. I'm surprised you haven't already had a heart attack. You've done some good in your life it seems, and God doesn't want you to go yet."

I was stunned.

"You should have died a long time ago," the doctor said. "But if you don't do something, your luck will run out."

It was so dire they wouldn't even let me leave the hospital. I'd probably need emergency open heart surgery.

I had some familiarity with heart surgery. Both my parents and four of my brothers suffered from heart disease, and most of them had undergone surgical intervention. I recalled my brothers Salem and Emad telling me about it. "It's awful. It's torture," they said. Not surprising considering how invasive it is—they literally saw through your ribcage and cut into your heart. It's a miracle modern medicine even has the capability; more miraculous still that a human being can survive it.

But you will come out of it scarred, in every sense of the word. Some of the people I've known who went through it, lost something. They gained weight or their attitude changed, becoming self-pitying or fearful.

I had to make a decision by next morning. I called three doctors I knew in the US and Lebanon. When I sent videos of the angiogram, they all recommended the surgery. I still wasn't convinced.

I asked to meet with the heart surgeon at the hospital. My friend and colleague, Maher, was with me in the room when we met the surgeon. This one also pushed for surgery. When the surgeon left, I said, "Didn't that feel like a sales pitch?" He agreed. It seemed like the surgeon had already made up his mind when he walked through the door and wasn't really listening to my concerns.

Time was running out. I scoured the internet for information and read about how stents—a metallic mesh tube that opens up the artery—are sometimes used as an alternative to open heart surgery. My brother Ali had opted for stents instead of an operation.

Not everyone is a good candidate for stents, though.

The next morning my doc came in. "Have you run a stent assessment?" I asked. He said he would.

An hour later he came back and said, "Yeah, you're eligible. Whether we do open heart or stents, the outcome is still going to be the same."

Without hesitation, I said "let's do the stent."

Implanting a stent still requires surgery, and surgery is always a grim prospect. Anything can go wrong. One of the blockages was in a very critical place and they had warned me there was a small chance operating on it could induce a heart attack. So, they had an open-heart surgeon present just in case they had to do emergency surgery.

You go in thinking, "Am I going to survive this?" My wife was terrified at the thought of losing me. We'd been together for close to 30 years. My kids were just scared and confused.

Well, I did survive, and as often happens when you have a near-fatal health scare, it inspired me to make some changes. I saw it as another chance from God to live well, stay healthy, and make the most of my time.

I was also determined to maintain a positive attitude. Instead of making me weaker, I became stronger.

But the ordeal raised some troubling questions. How did an otherwise healthy man develop such grave cardiac problems at a relatively young age? Clearly, family history was one factor. But the main cause, I suspected, was stress.

For basically the last 7 to 10 years I had been operating in a high-stress environment. Kitchens are strenuous. Hotel front offices can be emotionally and mentally taxing too. But all that seems quaint compared to the high-octane pressure of the corporate environment. Long hours, frequent travel, office politics, the competitiveness of the industry, the expectations to meet ever-higher expectations—it all adds up.

I wore a blood pressure monitor and found that my BP was highest during work hours. That was empirical proof that the job was adversely affecting my health.

But what could I do with that knowledge? I had to talk to a friend. Over a cup of coffee at Alchemy Cafe, a hip, minimalist spot that was one of our favorite hangouts, I told JJ how I was faring and reflected on the toll that work was wreaking on my body.

JJ never minced words—he was a straight shooter. "To hell with the job. Don't sacrifice yourself for the company. Life is short. You've gotta take care of yourself."

He advised me to ease up on my rigorous travel schedule.

"That's saying a lot, because you're on the road even more than me," I said.

"Don't worry, my friend, I've got a plan. In two years, I'm retiring," said JJ.

Retirement wasn't even on the radar for me; I aspired to do more. There was so much I had yet to achieve, stress or not. But I was happy for JJ that he would be exiting soon, a timely close to a distinguished career.

Meanwhile, I took great care to protect my health while avoiding unnecessary medical intervention. For me, and I believe for most people, the best cure is prevention. Your body is engineered to be resilient, if you care for it. I was always skeptical of the medical system and physicians in general. My experience with the artery blockages only sharped that skepticism. They should have caught it, and they should have informed me that stents were an option, without me having to do all the research.

I wasn't bitter about it, but I was more careful to advocate for myself, stay informed, and not take anything a physician says as gospel, especially the first opinion. Get a second, third, or fourth opinion. Don't be afraid to challenge doctors. They are human, and not always right, even the good ones.

For example, I really don't want to have to take medicine daily. I try to avoid it. At one point I was prescribed eight different types of pills. Instead of just gulping them all down unthinkingly for years on end, I did my research and asked the doctor to explain the purpose of each one. He agreed that I could probably work on improving my results for each medication and then we could do without some. We reduced the regimen from eight pills to three, and for some we reduced the dosage by half. It was a long process, of course, and I worked with my doctor to make sure I was doing everything responsibly. You can't just decide to stop certain medication.

A few months later, JJ was in Jeddah again. We had plans to meet in Dubai the next morning, after he returned. His last night in Jeddah, he posted a photo on Instagram of him and his team at the Hilton. JJ had this habit where he would post selfies with his team every time he visited one of his hotels and would hash tag it #SelfiewithJJ. In that pic he looked somewhat tired and he was not clean-shaven as he usually was. Travel fatigue, I figured.

I left a comment: "Are we still on for breakfast?"

"Of course," he replied.

The next morning, I showed up at our usual spot, Bull & Bear at the Waldorf Astoria Dubai. At five past the hour, I checked my watch. JJ was late, a rarity for a man who unfailingly showed up early. Ten more minutes passed, and I messaged him on WhatsApp: "Guess you're not coming. I'm going to order breakfast and you're picking up the bill!"

I drove back to the office, a bit concerned. Minutes after settling into my desk, my phone rang.

"Haitham, Aligi here." I knew Aligi from my days at Hilton as well. "JJ passed away in his sleep last night.". Like with my own health crisis, no one saw it coming. But he wasn't as lucky as me. Fate got to him first.

I froze, trying to process what I just heard as I looked out over the Dubai skyline; skyscrapers full of office workers on calls, ordering lunch, the roads and highways full of cars zipping around. An otherwise ordinary day. It is strange how in the face of death, life keeps on turning. In an instant your whole world is altered, but the world around you continues on, blissfully unaware.

JJ passed on April 28, 2023, just 18 months from his planned retirement. A man who was healthy, fit, well liked, and loved life. And just like that, on an evening like any other, he slipped into bed next to his wife, turned out the light, closed his eyes, and never opened them again.

GONE BUT NOT FORGOTTEN

JJ was an exceptional human being. A caring, trustworthy person who loved people and was passionate about his job. A true friend and steadfast confidante. He had an impressive CV but you would never know it from his modesty. He never felt he was above anyone. Never thought he was too good to stop and take a selfie with a steward or chat with the dishwasher (the kind of thing he did often.)

In the tight-knit world of hospitality, the news traveled fast, prompting an outpouring of praise and remembrances from those JJ touched, including many colleagues in the hospitality business. "A true friend who will always hold a special place in our hearts." A "true hotelier full of passion, presence, and pride." A humble and honest family man, "full of courage and strength."[5]

I wrote a tribute of my own: "It is painful to lose a dear friend; I am still trying to come to terms with the loss of JJ. His sudden departure is a huge loss to me personally and all those who knew him. He was a remarkable man, an inspirational leader and had been a great friend to me all these years. I will miss him deeply. Rest in peace, JJ. You will never be forgotten."

The shock impacted me greatly. It was one of the lowest points in my life. Besides the grief, it also hit me with some heavy, existential questions, as death tends to do. What am I doing? What am I working for? I enjoyed my career

---

5   Josh Corder, "Tributes pour in for 'passionate and inspiring' Jochem-Jan Sleiffer," Hotelier, May 1, 2023, *https://www.hoteliermiddleeast.com/people/ tributes-pour-in-for-passionate-and-inspiring-jochem-jan-sleiffer*

tremendously. I was grateful for what I had. And I relished being able to provide a good life for my family.

But I couldn't help feeling that much of what I did day to day was driven by the wrong reasons. Appeasing shareholders, delivering more and more for the company, dealing with pressure to cut costs, driving the top line, expanding the number of hotel rooms, increasing the share price. The ceaseless pursuit of growth for growth's sake.

I'm hardly the only one who feels this way. Many of us, maybe all of us, are caught in this web. Society itself is driven by a quest for more, more, more. Some economists will tell you that capitalism cannot sustain itself without growth. Is this healthy? Obviously, we all want to improve. We want to do better this year than last, and better still next year. We want to enjoy a good life, with comfort and maybe a little luxury here and there. But there is a point when it just becomes too much. If you're living to work, not working to live, it's a problem.

I've had record results with this company ever since I first joined years ago. I had the numbers to prove it. I was proud of my contributions. But I nearly died! And my dear friend *had* died. We can't say for certain what caused his cardiac arrest, but I am sure that job stress contributed to it.

I won't ever forget that life is short, and you must spend it doing what really matters. A cliché, yes, but like all cliches it comes from a fundamental truth. In Arabic there is an expression: *Alwaqtu kālssayfi in lam taqṭa'hu qaṭa'aka. Time is like a sword; if you don't cut it, it will cut you.*

JJ also understood that. He was getting ready for the next phase of his life, the post-work phase. Unfortunately, time had other plans. It cut him down too soon.

A year after JJ's passing, I attended the Future Hospitality Summit in Riyadh. It was poignant because during the previous one, JJ and I were on a panel together. I missed him on this occasion and shared the stage with his successor. No one spoke of JJ, and I realized that his team from Hilton had moved on. That's what life is about—you *have* to move on. You can't linger on the bad things. And his legacy still lives on amongst his friends and fans. But it was bittersweet, and it drove home the lesson for me that even if you dedicate every waking moment to work, when you're gone, the only ones who will continue to remember you are your family and friends, those close to you.

Today, when I hug my kids, or listen to a beautiful piece of music, or get together to break bread with my brothers and sisters, or simply wake up to face another day, I am reminded of what is important. The sword of time is like any weapon, a form of power: you can be cut. Or you can pick it up and wield it to create the life you want.

CHAPTER 9

WE HOPE YOU ENJOY YOUR STAY

JJ's passing, and my own health crisis, forced me to confront a lot of big questions about life, work, family, and ambition.

I had to take care of myself. But I was also driven to succeed.

So I did what I knew best—I got back on that bike. I kept cycling.

It wasn't easy to keep up the pace. But in the next year, my team and I beat our own records and we bested most of our competitors, according to external audit reports.

In the third year, we did it once more.

We were rolling, but my health scare drove home the fact that there was a hidden cost to all this driving for performance.

I thought maybe it was time to prioritize myself, which I hadn't ever really done. I owed it to myself, my family, and my employer, to stay healthy. I'm still trying to find the right balance while surging ahead and making each year better than the last.

I would like to say that my brush with death, then JJ's demise, precipitated a major change in how I lived. That's the movie version. In real life, change rarely occurs so easily or so suddenly.

The truth is that I am a selfless person by nature, and I've found it hard to be a little more "selfish." But at least, I am taking better care of my health, and putting aside a little more time to do things that give me joy.

As soon as I get to the office it's boom boom boom, one thing after another. Most days I'm eating lunch at my desk, often while simultaneously conducting a meeting. My hours are filled talking and listening, solving problems, creating ideas, launching initiatives, and at the end of the day, I'm drained.

So, I've come to appreciate the moments of restful solitude. There is great pleasure in being by yourself, and a big difference between being "lonely" and being "alone." Sometimes just a few moments of alone time, whether it's reading, walking in nature, or simply sitting and reflecting, are enough to restore me.

Would I like more free time and less stress? Of course. I'm getting there. It's a long-term project. I'm going to have to be patient.

THE VALUE OF HOSPITALITY

Travel binds us as a civilization. People don't want to stay sealed up in their little cocoon. We want to see the world and to connect with others beyond our own environs. Whether that means journeying to the next town for the day, taking a weekend getaway to a neighboring city, or embarking on an epic adventure around the world, the motive is the same. We are curious creatures who like to roam. But we also have a powerful need for comfort, belonging, and safety—all the hallmarks of "home."

That's the function that hotels fulfill. A place that lets us travel, explore, celebrate, and connect, while guaranteeing we have somewhere warm and secure to lay our head at night.

Maybe I'm overstating things a little, but I do believe that the continued progress and well-being of our species depends on hotels running. Without them, there is no travel, there is no venturing to the next frontier, there is no reaching across borders, boundaries, cultures, and communities to build bridges, share ideas, make connections, and simply enjoy life.

And I'm proud to be part of this industry and play a role in keeping the lights on, wherever you might be, however late you might check in, whatever you need to enjoy your time there.

I grew up in hospitality. I started when I was 17. More than three decades later, I'm still here. It's pretty much the only thing I know. The hotel business is my life.

My passion for the industry was sparked during my first days as a dishwasher and has never stopped growing. With the steam blasting my face and the detritus of dinner dirtying my uniform, I never imagined that one day I'd be in the top tier of a premier hotel chain, hobnobbing with ministers and monarchs, and negotiating deals with high-net-worth investors in the most glamorous hotels in the most exotic destinations in the world.

Well, take that back. I did imagine it. Not quite in the way it has manifested. But I knew I wouldn't be a dishwasher for long.

With each promotion, that passion grew.

With each new problem solved, I sought to tackle the next one.

With each new environment, whether a new team, a new hotel, or a new country, I relished the challenges and opportunities that came my way.

A lot of people who enter the industry will never advance past whatever position they have on Day One. And few persist for decades. I credit my resilience to being able to persevere. A German colleague once told me, "Haitham is like a German soldier. Every time he falls, he gets back up!" Of course, a German *would* compare me to a German soldier!

That's been my guiding light. When you stumble, find your footing. When you struggle, keep your head up and fight through it. Resilience has empowered me to survive the ups and downs of life and career, from the difficult but hopeful days as a young man who could barely keep the lights on in his rented apartment, to landing a sales and marketing leadership role responsible for literally half the world. From Eastern Europe, to Turkey, Russia, the Middle East and Africa. To rising through the ranks while fending off the twin-headed dragon of doubt: doubt from others and, more powerful, self-doubt. And, more recently, when my resilience enabled me to recover from a health crisis that could very well have been fatal.

Grace under pressure. Whatever you endeavor to achieve in life, remember that. That's your strength.

Depending on where you're at in your career, you might fear you are mired in a "sea of sameness." There are so many others in your position: how do you stand out in order to be given that next big break? The truth is that, except in rare cases, it won't be *given* to you at all. You must create the opportunities that allow you to ascend. Make yourself useful, do everything with dogged persistence, provide creative ideas that solve the problems of those around you, and don't settle for mediocrity.

In every job I've used the same method: what can I contribute in my first 90 days? How can I make my mark? That's served me well.

Push yourself. Even when you don't want to. Especially when you don't want to.

You have to have a sense of service to others and to make yourself available—and if you're working in hospitality, you won't get far without this quality. Service is the essence of the business, from the CEO all the way down.

As you approach work with passion, you'll discover what really makes you tick: what you thrive on *and* what you're good at. This will be your areas of expertise, your specialization. You won't get far by merely being a generalist. You differentiate yourself by excelling at one or two things that few others do.

If you want to succeed, you must be known for something. Your superpower. Colleagues recognize me for my talent in multi-tasking, a problem solver with strong instincts and a decisive nature. Leaders cannot waffle. Leaders must choose. Not every choice will prove to be the right one. But indecision is detrimental. Execute, wait for your expectations to bear fruit, and if things turn out differently from how you anticipated, deal with the consequences.

Find out what your own superpower is and keep working on that to differentiate you from everyone else.

Develop your IQ AND EQ and have empathy and respect for people you work with. If you have EQ it's like a sixth sense. Like being able to read minds. Make a genuine effort to understand people.

Corporate environments can be cutthroat, and it only gets more competitive as you ascend to the top. In your career, you will likely be fending off rivals on all fronts: those above you who have the power, those below you who want your job, and those on your level who may not have your best interest at heart. But don't fixate on your enemies (who, to be honest, are few in number). They're not the ones who determine the arc of your career.

It's the friends and allies you cultivate along the way who will keep your boat afloat in stormy seas.

How do you build relationships over the long term? The cliché networking advice is to not talk shop but to "ask people about themselves." That's only half-right. You can't treat people as a means to an end; you have to take a genuine interest in them, regardless of what they might be able to do for you. The "ask them questions about themselves" routine is too often done with the wrong motives and turns into an interview or worse, an interrogation. Have you ever been cornered at a networking event by someone who bombarded you with question after question? It isn't pleasant.

There's no shortcut. Relationship building must be done organically, sans agenda, with *genuine interest* in that person. Finding commonalities. Not following some guidebook that teaches you how to conceal your real motivation.

Show a keen interest. That sparks a conversation. A conversation leads to dialogue. And dialogue grows into a relationship. Maybe even a friendship.

And what comes next? My big career goal is to become a global CEO. Right now, I'm at the regional CEO level. But I'd love to take the top perch and oversee a premier hotel company's worldwide mission.

I hope it's with IHG, but I'm open to the possibility that it might be with another firm. I'm a company man, and loyal, but here's the fact: you must be loyal to yourself first. Loyalty is not always reciprocated. I often say that I love my job, but my job needs to love me back equally.

That's good advice to the younger generation, though perhaps unneeded. Truth is, I think they grasp this better than my generation did when we entered the workforce. The love of your job is not unconditional. They might value you, but you are almost certainly not indispensable to them. Employment is a marriage of convenience, not love. It is not cynical to say so; it just recognizes the dynamic and how both parties—employer and employee or manager—can benefit each other.

I think of the armies of hotel workers who were let go in the early days of COVID, including people who had been there for years. Some of them felt so jilted they left hospitality with a chip on their shoulder, and never looked back. I remember a conversation I had with one former hotel employee: "They kicked me to the curb when I needed them most." It's a bitter pill.

Anyway, I'm happy where I am now. I'm not actively chasing a promotion. If and when the opportunity comes, I'll be ready. That's been the story of my whole career. I've never really gone out in the open market and cast a line and hoped for a bite. I've just done my best at the job at hand and waited for a great firm to recognize my efforts and the positive impact I can make on an organization.

Then something would come up and my gut would tell me, "That's for me. That's the next step."

Eventually, I'll retire from hospitality, but I don't want to just end up a couch potato, loafing around or playing golf all day. Perhaps I'll pursue a second career. I always had a fascination with dentistry. Once upon a time I considered it, but I was discouraged by how many years of schooling you need. But who's to say I can't become a dentist at 65 or 70?

Maybe there's a business idea there, combining two areas of expertise in one: hotels and dentistry. A hotel that houses a dental clinic in its lobby? (I've actually seen it). Or a dental clinic with the added luxury, comfort, and convenience of a hotel? Who knows?

There's always room for fresh ideas in this business, though it's funny if you think about it. The basic concept of a hotel hasn't changed much since the first inns centuries ago provided simple lodgings, a meal, and a welcoming spirit to weary travelers.

TODAY'S PROBLEMS, TOMORROW'S VISION: CHALLENGES FACING THE INDUSTRY

Hospitality, globally, is a vital industry. It's no exaggeration to say that the world depends on it for both business and pleasure. In and of itself, the sector is a major source of tax revenue and employment worldwide. But it also has an auxiliary benefit for other industries that depend on hotels to host business travelers, stage conferences, organize meetings, and network. Without hospitality, there is no business travel.

The same goes for hospitality-adjacent sectors such as tourism. If there's nowhere for them to sleep, you can forget tourists.

But the industry is facing challenges. In order to keep hotels serving guests and function as a cornerstone of the world economy, we need to meet those challenges head on.

WORKFORCE PIPELINE

When I started in the business, a lot of people my age went to work for hotels or restaurants in a hotel. Most folks did it for a year or two, but some stayed on and made a career of it.

I think young people today are less attracted to the profession, which is struggling with a labor shortfall in pretty much every market. For example, in the United States, two-thirds of hotels report difficulty staffing open positions.[6]

Every industry needs fresh blood to ensure it progresses. Generation to generation, younger people entering the workforce, in their teens and twenties, fill open positions, replace retiring employees, and inject vitality and new ideas. But if that pipeline runs dry, the industry withers.

There are several factors accounting for the labor bottleneck. During COVID, droves of hotel and restaurant workers were either laid off or quit. Many of them found other (often better) careers elsewhere and never came back.

It's also a matter of workplace culture. Younger millennials and Generation Z crave a more relaxed, flexible culture, one that caters to the needs of individual employees rather than the employer. They want weekends and holidays off, but hotels run 24/7/365, so entry-level workers often end up pulling shifts on Saturday nights and Christmas Day. When other fields offer perks like remote working, generous PTO, or even, as some businesses are now experimenting with, four-day workweeks, hotels can't offer that. It's financially and logistically unfeasible to staff a hotel on four-day shifts. You'd need to hire more personnel to cover

---

6   American Hotel & Lodging Association, "67% of surveyed hotels report staffing shortages," Feb. 2024, *https://www.ahla.com/news/67-surveyed-hotels-report-staffing-shortages*

the "missing" days. And good luck coming up with a way to let doormen or housekeepers work remotely!

I also perceive a generational shift in how younger people approach service as a job; namely, they don't view it as an "art" or a passion. High school and college grads don't want to serve others. They want to go into tech, healthcare, business, finance, STEM, or law, which to be fair tend to pay more than hotel jobs. Ironically, many of these professions also involve serving, albeit in different ways. But, maybe, the hotel business doesn't have the same cachet.

One selling point for attracting talent is that the business does provide a career path, which is elusive for many young people. If you work for a big chain, there will be opportunities for growth. And there are many entry-level roles for folks who don't have a degree.

I'm an example of how you can start in one department and work your way up, through many different jobs. Many of my colleagues have followed the same path. We started on a lower (sometimes the lowest) rung of the ladder and advanced. So, the business does offer a career track and, perhaps, more job security than in other fields: if you're talented and ambitious, you can advance vertically, laterally (moving to other hotels within the organization), or perhaps geographically—skills translate well region to region. My own experience is testament to that: I moved seamlessly from Atlanta to Orlando to Dubai.

The caveat is that the way to the top is not *easy*. At every stage you're competing with a large number of peers for a limited number of promotions. This is true of most industries, but as a counterexample, a high-skilled tech worker can probably jump easily between companies, at least when the market is healthy, and net a big pay boost. It's not so simple in hotels.

In a hypothetical hotel of 100 rooms, you might have 150 employees. A handful are the senior leadership, maybe fifteen are the managerial staff, and everyone else is essentially equal! Yet, most of the folks at the bottom covet the same thing: promotion to the next level. It can be challenging to stand out—especially when you're all literally wearing the same uniform! These barriers are present in any industry, and any large company, but the challenge seems particularly pronounced at the lower levels of a large hotel.

It could take years, or even decades, for a new employee to make headway, and young people have not traditionally been known for their patience. Respectfully, the lack of patience is more acute today in a generation raised on the high-tech convenience of instant gratification: push a button and you get what you want.

By the time they finish college, they feel entitled to a good job and eschew entry level positions in a hotel, which might take ten years of hard work before you really get into a prestigious position.

So, what's the solution? At the hotel level, "in the field," we need to change our thinking and culture to allow the younger generation to take on more responsibility and management roles even without experience. Instead, assess candidates based on education, character, adaptability, and potential. Identify the future stars with raw talent and develop them. But that's going to require a major shift in mindset.

At the upper level and in the corporate side of things, we should probably be more open to youthful interlopers displacing some of the old guard. In tech, 30-year-old CEOs are normal. In the hotel business, a hotel GM has to go gray before they're respected. Perhaps I'm comparing apples to oranges, but the more we cultivate a youth-friendly culture, the more likely we are to attract the next generation of talent.

For example, a young woman I know, Isabel, has accelerated her career to become a leader in the IHG organization. She has a rare combination of drive, commitment, and tenacity, and has always shown strong commercial acumen and understanding of hotel operations. She is well liked, built strong relationships with the owners and earned the respect of employees.

That kind of talent is uncommon, but it does exist. Upper management should look for other Isabels in-the-making, waiting in the wings for their chance.

HIGH-TOUCH VS. HIGH-TECH

I had a strange experience recently on a trip to Berlin.

From the moment I entered the hotel to when I kicked off my shoes and settled into my room, I didn't interact with a single human being. There was no doorman at the entrance. There was no concierge at the front desk—in fact there wasn't a front desk at all. No bellhop or bartender or any human employee at all. I know there was housekeeping staff lurking about, but they were like ghosts the entire time. When I requested an extra blanket, I didn't speak to anyone or call anyone (there was no room phone anyway), I did it through an app. I'm not even sure the customer service agent I spoke with on the app was a person. It could just as well have been a chatbot.

This hotel is an experiment—a stripped-down operation that automates and digitizes everything from checking in (done in advance) to handling luggage storage, to giving you "keys" (just a code on a keypad) for your room. And we're the guinea pigs. I can't say I particularly enjoyed the experience. The absence of the human touch made my stay rather cold, soulless, and "mechanical," like I was just part of an assembly line. But it might be a harbinger of things to come.

One day, we might even be staying in hotels that aren't staffed by people at all.

High-touch vs. high-tech is the big debate among not just hoteliers but in many fields. Advancements in digital and mobile technology have allowed us to automate and do things faster, more efficiently, and with fewer errors, replacing human workers and in some cases entire occupations (such as certain data entry clerks). But counterintuitively, faster, more efficient, and more accurate does not always equal *better*, especially for functions for which clients are accustomed to the high-touch, personal service, provided by actual human beings.

Moreover, despite the buzz surrounding technologies like "artificial intelligence," humans invariably do some things better than even the most sophisticated piece of software. Socializing, understanding the nuances of language, navigating cultural and linguistic gaps, showing emotion and empathy, abstract thinking, and creative problem solving remain the purview of actual people. And these skills are vital in hotels, particularly in guest-facing roles.

These experiments are not the stuff of the future; they're playing out in real time. For example, a hotel in Silicon Valley introduced robo-room service, whereby a humanoid bot will navigate to the guest's floor, motor down the hallway, announce its presence at the door, and deliver the ordered food or drink item.[7] It can also supply towels, toiletries, or meals ordered on a separate app like GrubHub.

Intriguing, but this strikes me more as a PR stunt or novelty than a sign of things to come. New technology is always accompanied by a lot of hype; promises of "revolutionizing" or "disrupting" an industry often fall flat. It's also not certain whether the economics really make sense. Robots don't draw a salary or need health insurance, but their up-front cost is significant and, while they don't take time off, they do break down. Repairing a high-tech piece of equipment is costly. And how does this arrangement work? Will a hotel have to train its own maintenance staff in robo-repair or does the robot's manufacturer take responsibility? Will it send a technician to the hotel right away or does the hotel have to ship it off to the factory? How do you fill the gap when the bot is out of commission? And who pays for all this? These logistical questions shed doubt on the apparent ease of newfangled tech solutions.

More importantly, do guests really *want* humanoid machines serving their drinks? Some guests might be titillated by the prospect. Some might be annoyed, or even horrified. They probably don't care either way as long as they don't have to wait long for the club sandwich or bottle of chardonnay they ordered.

My sense is that customers want whatever makes their stay comfortable without increasing the cost—what that means in practice is to be determined. But no one is really *clamoring* for a roboticization of functions that are done by people.

---

7   David Louie, "Robots filling in staffing shortages at some Bay Area hotels with no tips expected," ABC7 News, Jan. 4, 2022, *https://abc7news.com/ robots-robot-hotel-silico-valley/11421841/*

Where customers desire high-tech, even at the expense of high-touch, is in the mundane or dispiriting aspects of travel and lodging, such as the check-in process. Online check-in is far from seamless and when it isn't implemented well, such as when guests who already provided their ID and personal info are asked to do it all again downstream, it makes things worse.

Most of us like to be greeted by a warm, smiling face when we arrive, a gesture that makes a hotel feel more like home. But we like it only if the check-in is easy and breezy. As a species, we loathe waiting in line. It's one of the features of a well-run hotel, whether it's a budget place or five-star luxury: don't make people wait.

There are times when I'm grateful technology has changed things and I don't have to interact with a person. For example, I'd rather not have to *call* room service on the phone. I prefer ordering on an app, where menu items are unambiguously displayed, and pay for it on the same app, without having to sign a check or anything. I'd still like my order to be delivered by a human being, but let's cut out all the other person-to-person interaction if we can do it just as well with a few swipes or taps.

The same goes with laundry. How marvelous that we can arrange dry cleaning or ironing with a few clicks on our smartphone—pickup time, drop off time, payment, all of it. And you don't even have to be *in* the hotel to do it. This is something privately owned laundry shops offer today. I'd prefer not to speak to the laundry department because the message gets lost in translation, often literally. Once on a business trip to China, I needed a suit pressed, so I rang down.

"Hi, is the laundry open?" I asked.

"Laundy open!" said the woman in Mandarin-accented English.

"Great, can you send someone? I'm in Room 511."

"Laundy open!"

"Yes, I understand. Can you please send someone?" She then said "one moment please" and transferred me to a different line.

"Hi, I just need a suit pressed," I said. "Can you help me?"

"Laundy no open!"

It makes much more sense to provide this kind of service via an app with a minimum of fuss, dialogue or human interaction.

Some hotels have adapted smart lockers to facilitate better laundry management, where guests can drop off laundry or dry cleaning 24/7. Their order is processed and the guest is transmitted status updates until their item is ready to be collected at smart lockers. This avoids the hassle of too much back and forth between the guest, reception, and laundry.

And robotic folding and sorting machines have made handling laundry even more efficient and less human-dependent.

Maybe the solution is more about digitizing steps rather than the whole process.

I often use the term "travel anxiety." From end to end, from booking to settling into your room, you deal with cumulative sources of aggravation. When you book, you stress about price and availability. When you pack, you fret about what to bring or wonder if the airline will charge for excess baggage. Dealing with airports and the flight itself involves its own sources of stress which I need not elaborate on. Then when you land at immigration, you hope your bags won't be combed through by overzealous customs agents looking for contraband fruit.

Finally, you leave the airport, but you still have to deal with transit to the hotel, traffic and language barriers. And, at the hotel, you just hope your reservation is in the system, you get the room you booked (and it has everything you were promised), and the hotel provides a peaceful respite, without the customary 3,000 yodelers gathering for a big convention.

Tech can relieve some of these burdens. But we must balance digitization with the human element. An element that has always been one of the central pillars of the hotel and restaurant business. Finding the right balance, in a way that also encourages growth in revenue and profit for owners, will be one of the big challenges facing hotel professionals in the decades to come.

VRBOH-NO: ARE HOMESTAY APPS A LONG-TERM THREAT?

A generation ago, the thought of short-term renting your living space to a stranger, or staying in a random person's house in lieu of a hotel, would have seemed bonkers. But apps like Airbnb and VRBO have certainly shaken the hotel industry and gobbled up a piece of the accommodation market share.

However, I don't see services such as Airbnb to be a significant threat, now or in the future.

The traditional hospitality sector is still enormous, and Airbnb is never going to displace it. There will always be people who prefer hotels because they like the hotel experience, not just a place to lay their head. Food and beverage offerings, concierge service, customer loyalty programs, the presence of a nice lobby, and so forth. Airbnb doesn't offer any of that.

There are other drawbacks to Airbnb. In the listings, what you see is not always what you get, photos and guest reviews notwithstanding. Sure, there are awful hotels too, but generally hotels are more thoroughly "vetted" by travel personnel, guidebooks, customer reviews, industry watchdogs, government agencies, and other stakeholders who in various ways check out a hotel and ensure that it's a suitable place to spend a few nights. Just to even *build* and operate a hotel involves a lot of steps and a lot of committed stakeholders and investors, in a way that implicitly suggests "This is a decent place to stay." Of course, none of this you see or even think about when you waltz into the lobby for a three-night jaunt. But in a sense, all these previous "inputs" serve as a tacit guarantee that the hotel is up to par.

None of that goes into an Airbnb. They are not hotels, but simply houses and apartments converted for hotel-like usage. One purpose does not necessarily translate to the other, especially when Airbnbs are essentially run by amateurs, not people trained in the profession. Now, I'm not going to claim that providing clean sheets and towels and managing check-in is some kind of secret, esoteric knowledge that only we hoteliers possess. That said, all it takes is one unpleasant stay in someone's messy two-bedroom apartment to appreciate the standards of service and professionalism that go into operating a hotel.

All this has contributed to a consumer backlash against Airbnb, as guests have grown tired of onerous fees, cleaning requirements, dubious and deceptive listings, and other inconveniences. Residents of cities who fear their way of life is imperiled by gentrification and rising housing costs have also taken aim at homestay companies for their role in converting housing stock to homestays for tourists. Some cities, such as Barcelona, Budapest, and Berlin, have passed laws significantly curtailing Airbnb's reach in an effort to put more homes back on the rental market for locals desperate for housing.

Consumer tastes, economic trends, and political winds are hard to forecast over a longer timeline. Perhaps the backlash will ebb, municipalities and tech companies will negotiate an agreement that satisfies everyone, and people will come to embrace homestay apps again. Or some other disruptor will emerge to challenge hotels.

But, for the time being, I'm confident that we, in the hotel business, can acknowledge Airbnb's importance while accepting that it provides a fundamentally different service altogether.

CRISIS MANAGEMENT

I'm more concerned with other types of threats: not competition, but some kind of global crisis.

Something like COVID, which is probably, but not certainly, a once-in-a-lifetime event. War, global depression, climate disaster, or some other industry-paralyzing pandemic could bring everything to a halt. We can't prevent such scenarios, but we can prepare for them. That's the difference between crisis and resilience. We don't want to be merely reactive to crises. In a resilience mindset, we anticipate crisis events and make plans to endure them.

Yet most big hotel companies have no real plan and simply hope they won't happen.

I'm a proponent of setting up a "crisis/resilience fund," where we sock a small percentage of revenue away each year as insurance against some crippling black swan event. This fund could allow hotels to stay afloat and allow for retainment of the workforce even during lean times, avoiding a mass exodus of human capital as happened in 2020-2021. Hotels already employ something similar, the FF&E (furniture, fixtures, and equipment) fund which ensures a reserve of capital for necessary repairs, upgrades, and renovation. In fact, many hotels tapped into, and in some cases depleted, their FF&E reserves during COVID, which underscores the utility of such funds.

A resilience fund is a "think big" expansion of that concept. So far, there has been lots of talk and little action. You'll hear conference panel guests and keynote speakers at industry events wax poetic about "resilience," but until resilience is supported by a plan, and brought into being through implementation, it's just a lot of hot air.

SUSTAINABILITY

Sustainability is another buzzword of the moment, and for good reason—no one can deny that our planet is in the throes of major environmental challenges. Challenges which may devolve into irreversible catastrophe if we don't take collective action. There isn't a single industry that isn't discussing how to make their business more eco-friendly. But dreams of reducing your carbon footprint are often stymied by difficult economic realities, and hospitality is no different.

We can, at least, agree that there is room for improvement. Hotels are an energy and resource-intensive enterprise, from keeping the lights on (24/7) and washing mountains of sheets and towels, to keeping rooms cool and pools heated. Restaurants that use single-serving plates and utensils generate large quantities of waste with every meal. Hospitality is responsible for one percent of global carbon emissions.[8] One percent might not seem like a lot, but that statistic translates into real-world impact on the environment.

This carbon footprint is significant, and it's going to take more than asking guests to kindly hang up their towel if they don't need a fresh one to really make a difference.

Sustainability is not just "the right thing to do," there's also a business case to be made for it. As a Deloitte study points out, the tumultuous effects of climate change sabotage supply chains, disrupt travel plans, impede business, and interrupt conventions and other events, all of which adversely affects revenue.[9]

Moreover, a growing number of consumers prefer to patronize companies that embrace a social and environmental ethos. In hospitality, branding is everything, and you don't want your chain to be perceived as the Halliburton of the hotel business.

But talk is cheap and solutions can be expensive. We must be realistic about what the hotel business can actually afford and what consumers are willing to pay. This requires honest discussions about who or what bears the brunt of sustainability-oriented changes.

If you want to go green, you've gotta spend some green. That harsh truth causes even the brightest-eyed eco-advocates to falter.

---

8   World Sustainable Hospitality Alliance, "Climate action," *https://sustainablehospitalityalliance.org/our-work/climate-action/*

9   Anjusha Chemmanur and Céline Fenech, "Sustainability in the hospitality industry," Deloitte, Feb. 14, 2024, *https://www.deloitte.com/uk/en/Industries/consumer/blogs/sustainability-in-the-hospitality-industry.html*

Surveys reflect a consumer desire to support sustainable hotels, but the same surveys also reveal that half of consumers say sustainable options are too pricey.[10] The reality is that when it comes to booking something, for most people, cost is going to win out over environmental concerns.

There are many green-friendly ideas being floated, but implementing them is the real challenge. For example, we can implement energy-saving measures in day-to-day operations and install solar panels on the roof. This type of change is an easier sell because it tends to save money (the less you spend on water, gas, and electricity, the happier the business managers will be—a win for everyone).

Other measures, like replacing plastic utensils and dinnerware with cutlery, or sustainable sourcing of food and beverage, are not so simple, because someone eventually has to cover this expense.

So, we're not short on ideas, but the bottleneck is an economic one.

Not one hotel company has come forward with an innovative way to measure individual guests' carbon footprint during a stay. Unless hotels install a meter for each room to show how many KWs or liters of water each room uses, we are not able to track guest consumption. The same goes with food consumption and waste.

Conveniences that hotel goers take for granted have an environmental impact. Televisions have a significant carbon footprint, yet every new hotel design has a larger and larger TV screen.

---

10   Kathryn Walson, "Consumers see costs as barrier to sustainable travel," PhocusWire.com, April 17, 2023, *https://www.phocuswire.com/consumers-see-sustainable-travel-costs-barrier-adoption*

Wouldn't it be amazing if we could show each departing guest the total amount of KWs, water and food they had consumed during their stay. Just to make them aware of their impact. And then, on the next visit, reward them for reducing their consumption.

Green hotels could absorb the cost of green initiatives instead of passing them on to the guest. That would make them more competitive, but in a privately-owned company, the profit motive overrules all else. Would the economic benefit of being branded the "affordable green hotel" offset the price of solar panels, reusable dinnerware, and on-site water recycling?

What should we do?

The industry must present a convincing story to owners/investors.

Of course, being a resident of Earth, like you, and a father who wants to preserve a livable planet for his kids and future grandkids, I favor environmentally friendly initiatives. I live in the UAE, which is especially vulnerable to the effects of climate change, due to rising sea levels, drought, dust storms, and extreme heat which could make our already scorching summers look like a cool August in the Scottish Highlands. But we have to be realistic about what is possible and not, simply in terms of economics and implementation.

There are nearly 200,000 hotels on Planet Earth (as many as 700,000 by some estimates)[11], [12]. About 17 million

---

11   Jordan Hollander, "75+ Hospitality Statistics You Should Know," Hotel-TechReport, July 9, 2024, *https://hoteltechreport.com/news/hospitality-statistics*

12   IBIS World, "Global Hotels & Resorts—Number of Businesses 2005–2030," Feb. 26, 2024, *https://www.ibisworld.com/global/number-of-businesses/global-hotels-resorts/1460/*

rooms.[13] According to the U.N., about a billion tourists took a trip in 2024, and that's just international visitors.[14]

However you measure it, there sure are a lot of people sleeping in a hotel tonight.

In each of those millions of rooms is a customer. A guest. A human being. Or several. Maybe they're on business. Maybe they're traveling abroad for the first time. Maybe they're a transplant who is new in town. A person between jobs, or between apartments, down on their luck, but hopeful for the next chapter.

Or maybe the room is empty, the guest checked out, the next one is yet to arrive. The bed is made up, the bathroom tiles sparkle, the curtains are drawn as the room sits in quiet repose, waiting for the next inhabitant.

Every visit is a story. Every stay is a quiet human drama that represents some small slice of a person's life. A story in which they leave home for a brief time, see or do something meaningful, then return to home. Every time I stay at a hotel, just before I lay my head on the pillow, the thought of who else has been in this bed before me crosses my mind. It could be anyone out there. Maybe someone I even know. The beds turn for different people from all walks of life, every single day.

And it's up to us to keep them turning, to keep the doors open, the minibar stocked, the breakfast and dinner plates full, and our guests happy. That is our driving mission. And I'm grateful to be a part of it.

---

13   IBIS World, " Global Hotels & Resorts—Number of Businesses 2005–2030," Feb. 26, 2024, *https://www.ibisworld.com/global/number-of-businesses/global-hotels-resorts/1460/*

14   UN Tourism, "Tourism Barometer," 2024, *https://www.unwto.org/un-tourism-world-tourism-barometer-data*

Printed in Great Britain
by Amazon